Finding Our Center

Wisdom from the Stars and Planets in Times of Change

Heather M. Ensworth, Ph.D.

iUniverse, Inc.
New York   Bloomington

Finding Our Center
Wisdom from the Stars and Planets in Times of Change

iUniverse books may be ordered through booksellers or by contacting:

Cover photos from NASA, courtesy of nasaimages.org

iUniverse
1663 Liberty Drive
Bloomington, IN 47403
www.iuniverse.com
1-800-Authors (1-800-288-4677)

Because of the dynamic nature of the Internet, any Web addresses or links contained in this book may have changed since publication and may no longer be valid.

ISBN: 978-1-4401-8392-8 (sc)
ISBN: 978-1-4401-8393-5 (ebk)

Printed in the United States of America

iUniverse rev. date: 11/20/2009

Awareness of an archetypal dimension of reality
and its intimate participation in human affairs
has over the centuries received perhaps its most
sustained and precisely articulated expression in
astrology.

Richard Tarnas, *Prometheus, the Awakener*, p. 3

Ah, not to be cut off… from the law of the stars.
The inner – what is it
if not the intensified sky.

Rainer Maria Rilke
(translated by Stephen Mitchell)

Contents

ACKNOWLEDGEMENTS

I am deeply indebted to all who have helped me to birth this book. I am grateful to Vicki Noble for inspiring me to study astrology. Joseph Crane and Dorian Greenbaum were instrumental in my astrological training. I am grateful to Bernadette Brady for her profound wisdom about the stars that helped to deepen my relationship with the sky. To Demetra George, I am indebted to her for her seminal work reweaving an understanding of the sacred feminine with astrology and mythology. I honor Carolyn Casey for her courage in bringing her astrological wisdom into the realm of culture and politics to encourage new ways of consciousness. Jeffrey Wolf Green has had a profound impact on my life and on my exploration of the spiritual dimensions of astrology. Judith Carpenter encouraged me through our deep and wide ranging conversations to translate my thoughts into writing. For all of these mentors and colleagues, I am deeply grateful. I am also thankful for the rich and supportive relationships that I have had with my astrology students and clients across the years who have stretched me intellectually, emotionally, and spiritually and have affirmed me in this work. I am also grateful to my friends and to the women's circles, which have so deeply shaped my life and path across the past two decades. For the ongoing love and support of my partner, Gail, words can not convey my gratitude.

The support that I have received for this book goes beyond the human realm. My ongoing, deepening path with Spirit has led me to this exploration of the meaning of the universe and of this time. I have also been forever changed by the mystery, wonder, and energies of the stars and planets as well as by the amazing complexity of life on this planet, Earth. I am honored to be in deep relationship with the Earth and sky and am filled with gratitude for their wisdom, guidance and transformative and healing presence.

INTRODUCTION

Since the beginning of human consciousness, dating back at least forty thousand years, cultures have questioned the meaning of life and formed an understanding of our relationship with the Earth and with the universe. The forms of these cosmologies have changed across time and across cultures. How are we to understand these ways of understanding life and the meaning of our existence? How do we become more consciously aware of the beliefs and values that shape our world in this time? In this time of intense global and environmental change, how do we find a deeper purpose and meaning that can guide us in how to live our lives?

We currently live in an intense time of transition and transformation. Many of us feel the increasing pace of time and the escalating tensions in our world. We have recently experienced a dramatic upheaval in our global economy. We are faced with ever-erupting global conflicts related to militant forces of nationalism and fundamentalism. We confront an increasing environmental crisis as we push our own and the Earth's survival to the brink of disaster. Hunger and famine are more widespread, and the gap between the world's wealthy and the poor is widening. Conflicts about nationality, ethnicity, gender, religious beliefs, and sexual orientation are rampant.

Individually, many of us feel that our lives need to change, yet we do not know how to do that or what that might mean. How do we make sense of this time of change and turmoil? How do we find our way in the increasing chaos and confusion of these times? Is there some larger meaning or purpose that lies beneath these crises? Where do we turn for answers?

In the midst of this cultural and personal turbulence, the religious institutions that have been a source of solace and of beliefs defining our sense of reality are showing signs of stress and fragmentation. The Catholic Church has been fraught with accusations of sexual abuse in the United States and Europe. The Episcopal Church is challenged by conflicting views about homosexuality and the confirmation of a gay bishop in the United States, which has erupted into worldwide dissension in the Anglican community. In the Middle East, there is an increasing division between nonviolent Muslim leaders and the militant fundamentalist groups. These are just a few examples of what is happening around the globe. What does it mean that the religious institutions and beliefs of the last two thousand years are in crisis? Where do we turn to find solace and spiritual guidance? Why are we experiencing such turbulent times?

Perhaps, if we view our current experience in the larger context of human history, we can gain clues as to what we are experiencing and how to navigate these intense times. In ancient cultures, there was a deep understanding that our lives are guided and mirrored by the movements of the stars and planets as well as by changes here on Earth. Across human history, the Great Year, the precessional cycle of 25,765 years in which the signs of the zodiac gradually shift in the sky at the time of the spring equinox due to the axial tilt of the Earth has given us guidance as to the evolution and shifts in our consciousness. Since ancient times, spiritual leaders and teachers have known that times of transition from one astrological age to the next are times of turmoil. Part of the turbulence of our time relates to the shifts in consciousness that we are experiencing in this transition from the Age of Pisces to the Age of Aquarius. Our ways of knowing, thinking, and formulating reality are being called into question.

Part of what is being challenged for us in this time is our view of the world in the context of polarization and duality. We tend to see life in dualities such as good/bad, light/dark, male/female, and self/other. We also see this polarization in our conflicting desires for connection and separation, for communion and control, for meaning and materialism.

In part, these dualities have resulted from an increasing split across the past few thousand years between our sense of self and other and our experience of spirit and body as well as the increasing split in our understanding of gender and in the relationships between men and women. This dualism has been fostered by the patriarchal consciousness of the past five thousand years and is exemplified in the philosophies of Plato and Aristotle and further refined by the work of Rene Descartes and the scientific revolution. Polarization has been codified in religious systems of thought that view the body as separate from spirit, and humans as set apart from nature. Nature becomes devalued and is something to be controlled. Women, in their intrinsic connection with nature in their monthly cycles and childbearing, have also been increasingly devalued in patriarchal society. But as we will see, this split has not always been evident in human history.

The dialectic of separation and connection is also evident in the history of our understanding of the human mind and in the development of psychology across the past one hundred years. Much of early psychological theory has been about the development of an individuated self (i.e., consider the theories of Freud and Jung as well as much of psychoanalytic theory). Psychological health was posited as the capacity to separate from merger (usually in relationship with the mother) and to develop an autonomous sense of self. To be a fully functioning person also meant having the capacity to contain and control one's feelings and impulses, to separate the mind from the body and emotions. Discrimination, analytical thinking, productivity, and many of the facets of left-brain functioning have been emphasized in modern Western culture. Intuition, imagination, holistic thinking and empathic attunement (aspects of more right-brain functioning) have been less valued.

In recent years, in modern Western culture, in developments in psychology and physics, we have begun to see a shift in this way of thinking. Recent psychological theories (such as the Stone Center Self-in-Relation work and developments in self-psychology and ecopsychology) have emphasized the importance of relationship in the formulation and maintenance of healthy human functioning. Dr. Allan Schore, who has written a seminal book, *Affect Regulation and the Origin of the Self*, links the effects of early emotional attunement and relationship to the neurobiology of early development and the subsequent development of the child's emotional and social functioning. Dan Pink, in his book *A Whole New Mind: Moving from the Information Age to the Conceptual Age*, states that effective functioning in our current time of change requires the skills, creativity, and flexibility of right-brain thinking that incorporate a more holistic way of being and knowing.

Developments in quantum physics are asserting what mystics have always known: that there is no clear demarcation between the observer and the observed, that there is no objective reality in the universe but rather that everything is interconnected. This sense of unity is inherent in our increasing awareness that a butterfly's wings may trigger a hurricane on the other side of the globe. Or, as recently occurred in the largest power outage in U.S. history, a tree falling on a wire in Ohio may trigger power failures across seven states and into Canada. All of life is interwoven. We can not separate ourselves from the larger whole, whether we are speaking of the global community, of the fabric of nature, or of our galaxy.

Environmentalists are calling us back to that awareness and reminding us that if we do not begin to live in more dynamic, respectful relationship with the plants and animals and landscape around us, we will destroy ourselves as well as our planet. Thomas Berry, among many others, passionately speaks of this in his book *The Dream of the Earth*. He has spoken of our need to understand this current time as the dawn of an ecozoic era when all of our political and environmental policies need to reflect the awareness that we are only one species among many inhabiting this planet.

Our increasing geopolitical awareness of being part of a global community also brings this point home. We are profoundly affected by the events in Afghanistan, Iraq, and the Sudan, and by the melting of the ice cap in the Arctic. We may try to isolate ourselves with nationalistic boundaries or, more locally, in gated communities, but there is no real separation from the realities of the world that we live in. This concept is also becoming more and more apparent economically. We may strive to foster and secure our own wealth and material comfort, but we find that we reap the consequences when we deprive others in order to better ourselves—in the instability of world markets and in the rise in terrorism in response to global injustice. We are becoming increasingly aware through compassion or through the consequences of our actions that we are not alone in this world. We are part of the global human community and part of nature. Each of us is a part of a thread in the web of the universe.

Our bodies and our psyches speak to us of this larger truth. Our bodies mirror our relationship to the natural world around us. As we overpopulate the globe, we find that cancer is on the rise. Cancer is the out-of-control multiplication of aberrant cells that spread through our bodies, bringing destruction to our organ systems. As we pollute our air and rivers, we find ourselves experiencing disorders of the immune system. Our cells turn against us as we have turned against the Earth. The more that we respond with increasing efforts to exert control (through warfare, consumerism, massive overdevelopment, etc.), the more we find ourselves faced with disease and the destabilization of our internal and external environments.

Psychologically, we have to wonder what it means that depression and bipolar disorder (i.e., emotional instability) are so rampant in modern Western cultures. Are these not in part a response to our increasing sense of disconnection from each other and from our natural environment and to the turbulence of these times? The prevalence of bipolar disorder may reflect the emotional and neurological stress of the profound changes in this time and the concomitant reorientation of our brain functioning (from left-brain dominance to more balanced hemispheric functioning).

Perhaps the widespread depression in our Western cultures is a manifestation of our growing sense of despair and disillusionment with our current ways of thinking and being. Perhaps some spiritual or subconscious part of us remembers that this is not the way that life has always been. We hear the faint whispering of our ancestral lineage reminding us of what it means to live in communion and in wonder, to be part of the larger whole. We remember what it was like to be in tune with the cycles of the seasons and the phases of the Moon. We remember when the movement of the stars and planets had meaning. We remember when we were a part of the fabric of life and knew the creative and loving energy that moves throughout the universe. We remember when all was one, and we were held in that knowing, in that fierce embrace.

How then do we find our way back into balance? Or is it even possible to go back? Perhaps, like the prodigal child, we need to return with the knowledge of what it means to experience ruptured relationship, the angst of separation and the despair of disconnection. Like the adolescent who defiantly asserts separation, we need to mature in the awareness that we are truly unique and whole only when we remember what it means to come back into right relationship—now with more respect and awareness of the profundity of our interconnectedness and the damaging results of defiance, illusory control, and separation. Perhaps, analogous to our individual psychological development, we have needed to move through this phase in our collective cultural evolution. But, like the acting-out adolescent, if we remain locked in this developmental stage, we will become increasingly destructive to ourselves and to all of life around us. We are being asked to engage in a profound shift in consciousness. We are called to move into more conscious communion and co-creation with each other and with the natural world.

But how do we return? How do we make this shift? Ironically, in recent years, as we become more aware of our increasingly fragile situation globally and environmentally, Western cultures have attempted to manage the problems through escalating efforts at control. We go to war preemptively to fend off the violence of war. We increasingly use antibiotics ("anti-life" pills) and toxic chemicals (chemotherapy) to "fight" illness. While these approaches are vital to the health and survival of many who are ill, they also reflect our dominant mentality of separation, aggression and control. Perhaps there are more options to recover our health and well-being. Perhaps war and dominance are not the most effective paths to world peace and stability.

We need to look deeper. We need to learn to listen. The increasing illnesses are giving us a message about our imbalance with nature and disconnection from our own bodies. The spread of violence and despair are speaking to us of global injustice and inequity. The rising greenhouse gases in our atmosphere are showing us that we are violating the very air that we breathe. The answer is not to try harder to assert control and dominance, but rather to pause and listen and remember what it means to be in right relationship. We need to return to attunement, to respect, to compassion, to an awareness of the interconnectedness of all of life. What we do to the rivers, we do to our own bloodstreams. What we do to our sisters and brothers in other countries, we do to our own children. What we do to the trees of the rain forests, we do to our own lungs. There is no separation. We live in a sentient universe, and we are a part of a unified cosmos.

In ancient times, our ancestors were more in tune with the meaning and wonder of the universe. They had an intrinsic understanding of natural law, and they lived in intimate relationship with the plants that they ate and used for medicines and with the animals that they hunted for food. They knew that their survival was dependent on being in right relationship, on interacting with other species with honor and gratitude. In native cultures, they understood that their actions in the present affected the seven generations to follow. For thousands of years, they knew how to listen to the pulse of the Earth and the songs of the stars. How then do we find our way back to that knowledge, not forgetting where we have been and who we have become, but coming back into relationship with the Earth, each other and all of life with more consciousness, wisdom, and respect?

Throughout human history, our cultural development has been shaped by the world around us and our relationship to it. This is evident in archeology and in mythology across the ages. What we have forgotten is how much our ancestors understood themselves as part of a larger whole. They knew that the currents that shape the universe also coursed through their veins and affected their lives. They looked to the patterns in nature and in the sky to guide them into more awareness of and attunement with the energy of the creative intelligence of the universe. They glimpsed the signature of the Divine in the cycles of nature, in the color or shape of plants, and in the movement of the stars.

Since the development of Newtonian physics and the industrial age, we have attempted to remove ourselves from that web of connection and have tried to analyze ourselves and nature as separate "objects" for study, dissection, and mastery. We have learned a great deal about the universe in this manner, but we have lost touch with a deeper sense of meaning and wisdom in the process. Our challenge is to begin to reweave our scientific understanding back into a cosmology, a sense of the meaning of who we are in relation to the cosmos.

Perhaps we can be guided by our ancestors in that effort. If we trace human history across the millennia, we will see that the patterns of culture and mythology were shaped by the movement of the stars in the sky, "as above, so below," not in a deterministic sense but in a relational context. This is the art and science of astrology, which has been in existence for thousands of years. In recent history, astrology has been devalued. We no longer seek meaning and wisdom from the sky but have focused on seeing the planets as bodies of matter to be explored and measured. It is time to reweave our collection of factual data with our ancestors' attunement to patterns, cycles, and a context of meaning. While we have blinded ourselves to the sky with our artificial light in our cities, the patterns of the stars and planets remain in the firmament above us. It is time to move beyond the analysis of our minds and to return to an opening of our hearts to the messages that the universe is trying to convey to us. The communication is there if we are willing to listen.

In this book, we will trace some of the themes of the ages of human history through looking at the precession of the equinoxes and how the shifting of the constellations in the sky has been reflected in the beliefs and developments in human culture. These themes will be presented in broad strokes. This book is not meant to be a detailed historical or archeological analysis. Rather, it is an effort to begin to reweave that web of connection, to see how the shifts in the patterns of the Earth and sky are mirrored in our human consciousness and cosmology. The Great Year, or full circle of the precessional cycle through the signs of the zodiac (approximately twenty-six thousand years), is similar to the ancient medicine wheel. We learn through going through the cycle and integrating the energies and wisdom of each of the signs. Eventually, we learn to step off the wheel and integrate the meaning of the whole. When we come to that awareness, we are able to disidentify with whatever age that we are in and come to the center, holding the diversity of who we are and of our collective consciousness. In listening to the astrological cycles of this time, perhaps we can be guided toward that more whole and centered way of being, and in so doing, become creative and conscious collaborators of our destiny.

PART ONE

SETTING THE STAGE

CHAPTER ONE

LIVING IN A TIME OF TRANSITION

We are currently in a transition time between ages. We are leaving the Age of Pisces and are on the cusp of a new age, the Age of Aquarius. Ancient myths and modern science teach us that such periods of transition are marked by global and social turmoil. These are times that are stressful for the planet from a geological standpoint and also from a cultural or sociological perspective and involve significant shifts in human consciousness.

The cycle of astrological ages is related to the precession of equinoxes. Our Earth revolves around the Sun and rotates on its axis. However, our view of the sky gradually shifts over time (one degree every seventy-two years) due to the precessional cycle. The traditional understanding of this gradual movement of the Earth's axis in relation to the sky is that the Earth has a slow, wobbling movement due to the gravitational pull of the Sun and Moon, resulting in the shifting of the Earth's axis over time.

The visible manifestation of this is in the gradual changing of the celestial pole and the slow shifting of the constellations in the sky. For example, in 3000 BCE, the polestar was Alpha Draconis, but now our polestar is Polaris. (See Figures 1 and 2 below.)

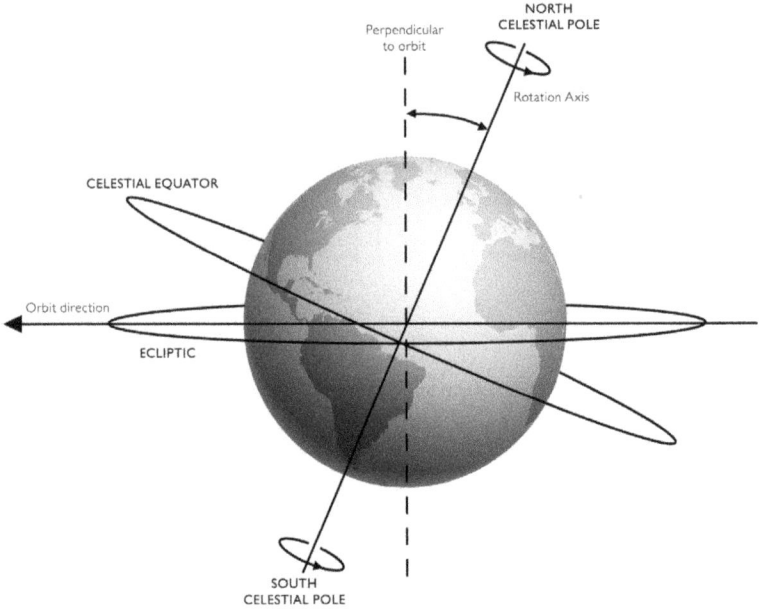

Figure 1: Tilt of the Earth's axis and the movement of the celestial pole

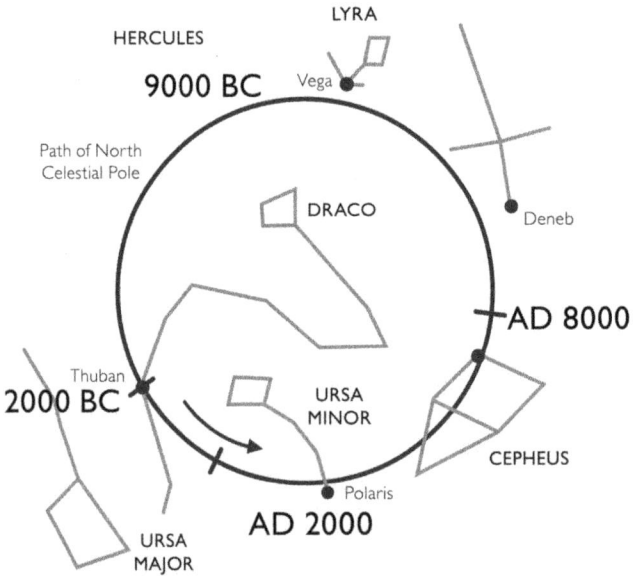

Figure 2: Change in polestar with movement of the celestial pole

About two thousand years ago, the constellation Pisces began to rise on the horizon at the time of the spring equinox, but now we are gradually moving toward the constellation Aquarius rising at that time of year. This shifting of the vernal rising of constellations is known as the precession of equinoxes. Each age lasts approximately 2,160 years.

Of significance is a recent different scientific hypothesis for the precessional motion proposed by Walter Cruttenden of the Binary Research Institute in his 2005 book, *Lost Star of Myth and Time*. A similar view has also been suggested by Dr. Richard Muller of the University of California, Berkeley, and Dr. Daniel Whitmire of the University of Louisiana. These researchers speculate that our Sun is part of a binary star system. This means that our Sun is gravitationally bound with another star, not yet identified, with both orbiting around a common center. Astronomers have noted in the past several years that binary star systems are common in the Milky Way galaxy. If this is the case, then the precessional motion is not due to the wobbling of the Earth's axis but rather due to our Sun's movement, which pulls our solar system in a gentle arc through space. The time that it takes for our Sun to complete one orbit would be the equivalent of the full precessional cycle (approximately twenty-four to twenty-six thousand years). As Cruttenden explains:

> Just as the spinning motion of the Earth causes the cycle of day and night, and just as the orbital motion of the Earth around the Sun causes the cycle of the seasons, so too does the binary motion cause a cycle of rising and falling ages over long periods of time, due to increasing and decreasing electromagnetic effects generated by our Sun and nearby stars.
>
> (Cruttenden, "Precession of the Equinox:
The Ancient Truth Behind Celestial
Motion," binaryresearchinstitute.org)

If in fact we are part of a binary star system, think how this would affect our understanding of the universe and of ourselves. Our overemphasis in modern Western culture on separation and individuation would be called into question, and in a deep and profound way, we would need to understand ourselves, our solar system, and our universe in a relational context.

Some of the researchers advocating the binary star theory believe that the star that we are orbiting with is the brightest star in our sky, Sirius. It is noteworthy that this star has been sacred in many ancient cultures. The Dogon culture in western Africa has honored Sirius for over five thousand years. Interestingly, long before the modern scientific discovery that Sirius is a twin star with Sirius A orbited by its invisible twin, Sirius B, the Dogon tribe worshipped both and were able to describe Sirius B as an invisible, heavy, but very powerful star. They believe that Sirius is the axis of the universe and the source of all life. In ancient Egypt, Sirius was worshipped for thousands of years (beginning about 3000 BCE) as the primary mother and life-giving goddess Isis, who was seen as the source of life and as the one who helped souls to incarnate on this planet. Many other ancient cultures honored Sirius as a primary deity. Perhaps these ancient cultures had knowledge that was subsequently forgotten in more recent times.

Whatever the cause of the precessional motion, it is significant and has been studied by humans for millennia. Initially, it may have been charted through the movements of the stars, particularly heliacal rising stars (i.e., those rising with the Sun) and the polar stars. Later, the constellations that follow the line of the Sun, Moon, and planets in the sky, the path of the ecliptic (about twenty degrees wide), were viewed as important markers of the seasonal cycle of the year and the larger precessional cycle. Many ancients referred to the planets as the "wandering stars," moving against the backdrop of the constellations. We know that the ancient Chinese and Babylonians originally developed a zodiac with six signs by the sixth century BCE. Later, about 630 to 450 BCE, ancient cultures created the zodiac with twelve signs, similar to the one that we use today (see Robert Hand, "History of Astrology – Another View," p.2).

While Hipparchus, a Greek astronomer who lived around 147 BCE, has been credited with the discovery of the precessional motion, many scholars believe that it was much more ancient in origin. Giorgio de Santillana and Hertha von Dechend in their seminal book *Hamlet's Mill*, describe how cultures around the globe and across human history have understood this slow, gradual process of the precession of equinoxes. These ancient cultures' astronomical knowledge of this phenomenon was embedded in their mythology, and these authors cite over two hundred myths from thirty different cultures around the globe, some dating back to the Neolithic (early prehistoric) period, that encoded numbers and references pertaining to the precessional cycle.

Many of these myths speak of this process as the "grinding of a mill," with the axis of the mill as the line reaching outward toward the polestar in the sky. These cultures often referred to the "four corners of the Earth," which are the world "pillars," or equinox and solstice points marking the framework of their world in that time. With the precessional motion, the framework of the world (i.e., the solstice and equinox points and the polestar) gradually shifts. Many of the myths from around the globe tie this shifting of the equinoxes and the times of transitions between ages as fraught with pain and danger. These myths associate images of "floods," "deluges," or cataclysmic disasters of some sort with these precessional changes.

In recent years, through scientific research, we have come to understand that the precession of equinoxes is also related to the patterns of glaciation and deglaciation. These periods of transition between ages have been associated with natural disasters that the ancients were attempting to warn us about. Scientists now know that the onset and retreat of ice ages are related to three factors in the Earth's orbital geometry: the obliquity of the ecliptic (which is the angle of the Earth's axis of rotation as well as the angle between the celestial equator and the ecliptic), the eccentricity of the Earth's orbit (i.e., the elongation of the Earth's path around the Sun, see Figure 3 below), and the axial precession (see Hancock, *Underworld: The Mysterious Origins of Civilization*, pp. 271-272).

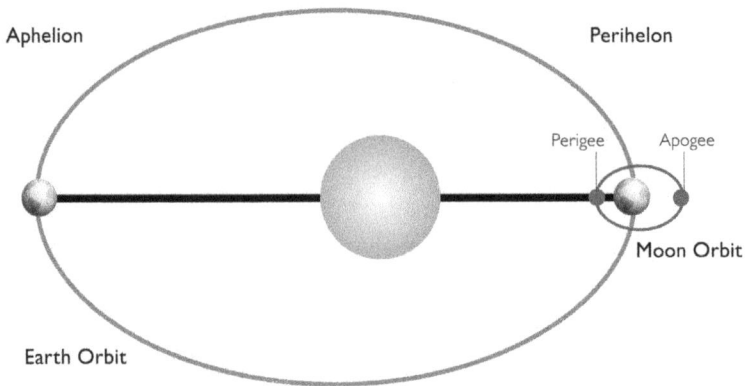

Figure 3: Earth's elliptical orbit around the Sun (from www.noaa.gov)

These factors affect the amount and intensity of sunlight and the patterns of global warming or cooling that lead to changes in the ice ages. What is important to note here is the level of sophisticated understanding on the part of ancient cultures about the gradual movements of the stars and how this had a profound effect on the world. Their myths were attuned to these patterns in the sky and their meaning for us on Earth in a way that we in modern times seem to have forgotten.

Not only does the precession of equinoxes cause changes in global climate patterns, it also relates to shifts in our social and political ways of being. Many ancient cultures viewed our development globally as cyclical rather than linear. These periods of advance and decline relate to the precessional cycle through the zodiac, or the Great Year. If in fact our precessional cycle is related to our being a part of a binary star system, Cruttenden and others speculate that these cycles may relate to the electromagnetic fields that our Earth moves through in space as we complete this approximately twenty-six-thousand-year orbit. Perhaps we advance in our consciousness and development as we move closer to the gravitational center of that orbit and decline as we move away.

Whatever the cause of the cycles, from a cultural perspective, these periods of shifting between ages are times of tumult as we let go of certain patterns of social, political, and religious organization and move toward new ways of being. Such periods are often characterized by a significant degree of backlash, or reassertion of the old forms in a more rigid and exaggerated manner in reaction or resistance to the process of dissolution and change. The forms that the backlash takes are shaped by the themes of the age that is ending. In our current time, for example, we are seeing an increase in terrorism arising from fundamentalist religious groups. These terrorists are often sacrificing themselves in a form of martyrdom for their religious cause. These are exaggerated expressions of the archetypes of spirituality and sacrifice that are characteristic of the Piscean Age.

In this book, we will examine in more depth the archetypal patterns of the astrological ages across human history and seek to understand the themes of these eras. We will look in depth at the Piscean Age of the past two thousand years and seek to understand the new ways of being that we are moving into in the Age of Aquarius.

This understanding of the archetypal energies inherent in the patterns of the sky and reflected in events on Earth is very ancient. Yet we are beginning to see this awareness resurface in our modern times. Richard Tarnas, in *Cosmos and Psyche,* traces the way in which this ancient attunement to archetypal patterns and to the sense of our living in a creative and intelligent cosmos was gradually lost following the Copernican revolution and the Enlightenment over five hundred years ago. He describes the way in which we now live in a narrowly defined world of "science" and a "disenchanted" universe. With amazing hubris, we assume that our capacity for creativity, consciousness, and symbolism are uniquely our own rather than being an extension and reflection of those qualities in the cosmos. He argues convincingly that we live in a sentient and meaningful universe, and that it is to our own peril for us to continue to blind ourselves to that deeper reality.

I would posit that the conflict between these worldviews, the one of the universe as a mechanistic "other" to be analyzed versus the cosmos as a relational context of meaning, purpose, and vast intelligence actually began as we moved into the patriarchal era (around 3000 BCE). This loss of connection with the sentient nature of the universe may also relate to the cycles of advance and decline related to the binary orbit of our Sun with its companion star.

According to the interpretation of the Hindu yuga cycle (i.e., the Hindu epochs associated with the precessional cycle), we are emerging out of the Kali Yuga, the lowest phase of consciousness in which people live in a materialistic manner with a primary focus on physical reality. According to this system, much of the wisdom of the past and energetic and spiritual understanding of the earlier ages is lost during the Kali Yuga or Age of Ignorance. It is a time of wars and of vying for power, with world leadership moving from being primarily in the hands of women to those of men.

According to the Indian yogi Swami Sri Yukteswar Giri (guru of Paramahansa Yogananda), the zenith of this twelve-hundred-year Kali Yuga phase was during the Dark Ages, or AD 500 AD. Since AD 1700, we have been moving into a higher phase of consciousness, the Dvapara Yuga. This yuga lasts twenty-four hundred years and is characterized by increasing scientific and spiritual understanding, awareness of subtle energies, and an understanding of the unity of all of life, as well as an increase in the prominence of the sacred feminine.

We will explore these shifts in consciousness in more depth in the coming chapters. As Tarnas notes, this ancient wisdom and renewed spiritual awareness began to resurface in modern times through Jung's depth psychology and his depiction of archetypes as principles embedded in our individual and collective unconscious. According to Jung:

> The content of the collective unconscious is made up essentially of archetypes. The concept of the archetype indicates the existence of definite forms in the psyche which seem to be present always and everywhere. Mythological research calls them "motifs" … This collective unconscious does not develop individually but is inherited. It consists of pre-existent forms, the archetypes, which can only become conscious secondarily and which give definite form to certain psychic contents.
>
> (Jung, *The Archetypes and the Collective Unconscious*, pp. 42-43)

This concept calls into question the Cartesian notion of "I think, therefore I am" and of the postmodern notion that all of our theories and understandings of the universe are based on the projections of our own thoughts and beliefs or that we have the capacity as individuals to shape our own reality. While we have conscious choice in our lives, we are also part of larger cosmic currents of change. The Jungian archetypes hearken back to ancient wisdom that we are in fact formed and shaped by the currents of an archetypal field that is beyond our control and beyond our full conscious comprehension. In attuning to that field and aligning ourselves with those larger forces and patterns, we not only come back into balance and right relationship with the life around us but also step into a greater sense of our own wholeness. As we face this crisis of transition, it is more critical than ever before that we see the nature of the universe and our own lives in a clearer and more holistic way rather than remaining blinded by our false presuppositions and by our disconnection from the world around us.

As we move through this time of change, we need to be aware of the phases inherent in such global and personal transformations. The anthropologist van Gennep, in his classic book, *The Rites of Passage*, stresses how major developmental shifts (whether individual or collective) are marked by certain phases of separation, transition, and then incorporation. Rites of passage parallel a death-rebirth process. We leave the old state, go through a transitional period, and then move into the new state or way of being. Ancient rituals and ceremonies celebrated these rites of passage and helped people through this transformational process. Today, unfortunately, in modern Western cultures, we have neglected this process and these types of transitional rites. In particular, we have minimized or repressed the critical importance of the liminal period, that time between the old and the new. This is a critical phase for releasing the old patterns and preparing or receiving initiation into a new form. In our movement away from a cyclical developmental view toward a more linear, exponential one, we have neglected this rich and important part of the change process.

The importance of the liminal period in cultural rites of passage is a reflection of the transitional phase that is a part of biological and cosmic rhythms. As van Gennep notes, it is a part of all biological and physical movement and activity in which you have periods of energy expansion followed by exhaustion and regeneration leading to a new phase of energy or movement (see van Gennep, p. 182). These cycles are also mirrored in the phases of the Moon, planetary movements, and even in the daily cycle of the Sun. They are also reflected in the seasons of the year and in plant and animal life. As van Gennep writes:

> Life itself means to separate and to be reunited, to change
> form and condition, to die and be reborn. It is to act and
> to cease, to wait and rest, and then to begin acting again,
> but in a different way. And there are always new thresholds
> to cross: the thresholds of summer and winter, of a season
> or a year, of a month or a night; the thresholds of birth,
> adolescence, maturity and old age; the threshold of death
> and that of the afterlife.
>
> (van Gennep, pp. 189-190)

What does it mean then for us to be on the threshold of this new age? How can we mark this rite of passage and move through it with consciousness rather than reactivity? What information can we garner from the patterns of the sky about what the themes of this new age might be? How do we honor the lessons of the former age, but prepare ourselves for the new forms, beliefs, and ways of being of the new age?

Rites of passage are ceremonial celebrations of transitions but also are acts of protection due to the awareness of the vulnerability of the individual or group during the tumult of the change process. Honoring the transitional or liminal period of unknowing, undoing, and dissolution (paralleling death) is a critical part of that protective process. This book will look at ways in which we can honor this liminal period and learn its critical lessons while we prepare for the changes that lie ahead.

CHAPTER TWO

SEEKING THE WISDOM OF THE PAST

Homo sapiens, modern humans, have been on the Earth for approximately forty thousand years. The historical period in which we have written records of previous cultures and times extends back approximately five thousand years. Prior to written records, we have the art and archeological evidence of prehistoric cultures to help us discern the traces of our past. What were we like in these earlier times and cultures? Much remains in mystery.

Erich Neumann in his seminal book *The Origin and History of Human Consciousness*, traces his understanding of the parallels between our psychological development and the unfolding of our human consciousness as manifested in our mythology. He believes that our prehistoric ancestors did not have a sense of ego or of self-consciousness but were rather merged in the sense of the oneness of all creation, much like the infant is with its mother. However, recent archeological and mythological evidence would indicate that this idea is not fully accurate.

In modern times, we hold to an image of human evolution and the development of human consciousness as a linear progression from primitive states to the more complex and advanced understanding of modernity. Yet an exploration of the wisdom of our ancestors shows the hubris and lack of veracity of those assumptions. Our concept of linear time is actually a recent development of the past two thousand years. Prior to that, most ancient cultures held to a cyclical view of time with periods of advancement and decline (such as the Hindu cycle of yugas).

In this book, we will, in broad strokes, explore some of what is known through archeology and mythology about the nature of human consciousness and culture across our recent development as a species. We will begin our exploration with a half turn of the precessional wheel, beginning in the Age of Leo (approximately thirteen thousand years ago). In part, we begin at this age because this is when human evolution and expansion increased significantly following the end of the last ice age. Also, as we will see in more depth later, this period has a significant relationship to the astrological age we are moving into now.

From an astrological perspective, we can chart these phases of our past in ages lasting approximately 2,160 years. These ages are named by the sign of the zodiac that appears on the eastern horizon at the time of the vernal equinox. The constellations of the zodiac, which mark the path of the ecliptic, have held meaning in cultures around the globe throughout human history. Ancient cultures believed that when stars touch the horizon, their energies incarnate and move among us. While different cultures have perceived their meanings in various ways, certain underlying archetypal themes emerge from the images and stories told about them across cultures and across time. These signs of the zodiac carry meaning and wisdom that live in our collective consciousness even when we have forgotten their stories and when we neglect to watch them move through the sky.

While we will trace these signs and their meanings across the millennia, it is important to note that we do not have written historical and mythological records for the period before 3000 BCE. For the period before that time, we have to attempt to decipher the beliefs and lifestyles of earlier peoples from the archeological record. We are able to find some of the shards of these earlier beliefs embedded in the oral traditions and later mythologies emerging from subsequent cultures in those geographical areas. We also are able to use the archeological record to gain insight into these earlier cultures.

A dramatic cultural shift occurred about 3000 BCE at the outset of our historical era. Archeologist Maria Gimbutas who has done extensive research on the prehistoric cultures of Old Europe, contends that this is when the ancient lineage of matrilineal and goddess-honoring cultures began to be supplanted by patriarchal culture. From the earliest archeological evidence (dating back thirty-five thousand years) up to approximately 3000 BCE, we find the predominance of goddess-worshipping cultures that used a lunar calendar for marking time. With the change into the patriarchal era (continuing up to the present), we moved from a focus on the Moon to one on the Sun and the development of a solar calendar.

In association with the prehistoric emphasis on the lunar calendar and Moon, Demetra George, in *Mysteries of the Dark Moon*, views the period of our human evolution as modern *Homo sapiens* across the past forty thousand years through the lens of the lunar cycle. In a complex and rich manner, she traces the shifts in our cultural and mythological patterns as correlated with the eight phases of the Moon (each equivalent to five thousand years of human history).

Within this model, the past five thousand years of the patriarchal period are equivalent to the dark Moon phase. During this time frame, the connection with lunar (and sacred feminine) consciousness became repressed. However, we are now on the cusp of a new era analogous to the new crescent Moon when the understanding of the sacred feminine is reemerging. This reemergence is evident in the increasing interest in women's spirituality as well as in the resurgence of ancient symbols from prehistory, such as the spiral seen in many advertisements. The images, symbols, and archetypal patterns of the ancient wisdom are resurfacing in our collective unconscious. This is a part of the larger transition that we are in at present.

As we explore the archetypal themes of the various ages and past cultures, we need to be careful not to project our own cultural assumptions and values back on those earlier times. In fact, it is very possible that the importance of the precession of equinoxes (and the constellations rising with the Sun at the vernal equinox) is of more importance in more recent solar cultures than it was in earlier times for prehistoric cultures.

Bernadette Brady has conjectured that the earlier cultures may have been more focused on the polestar, the still point in the sky, rather than on the movement of the constellations. She also has emphasized that in earlier times, the "canvas of the sky" was seen as having themes filling whole sections of the sky, "rather than as isolated images with isolated stories," as became more prevalent in later times (particularly from the time of ancient Greece to the present) (Brady, *Brady's Book of Fixed Stars*, p. 47). While the images associated with the current zodiac find echoes in mythologies around the world and across thousands of years, we can only speculate as to how they were interpreted in the prehistoric period.

CHAPTER THREE

THE WORLD TREE: THE MILKY WAY, GALACTIC CENTER, AND CELESTIAL POLE

Before we begin to explore the archetypal meanings of the astrological ages, it is important that we see this cycle in the larger context of our relationship with the universe around us. We reside on a planet on the outer portion of the Milky Way, our galaxy. Our Milky Way is a spiral galaxy, one of many in the universe. Our Sun lies about two-thirds of the way out from the center of this spiraling cloud of stars and gas. When we look up into the sky, we can see the white band of countless stars of our Milky Way stretched across the sky. Many ancient cultures viewed the Milky Way as the "World Tree." The World Tree throughout world mythologies has been seen as the connection and stabilizing bridge between the Earth and the sky. The World Tree, or Tree of Life, was thought to hold all of life in balance and alignment. We see references to this idea in the ancient Mayan culture, in the Hebrew Bible ("the Tree of Life"), and in the ancient Sumerian creation myth, among many others.

Another image (see Figure 4 below) that has resonated in our consciousness since prehistoric times is that of the cross. Many ancient cultures were aware that the line of the ecliptic, the path of the Sun and planets, intersects the Milky Way, forming a cross. The image of the World Tree, holding our world in balance, may relate to this cross formation and our integral relationship with the path of the Milky

Way. Amazingly enough, these two lines meet near the center of our galaxy.

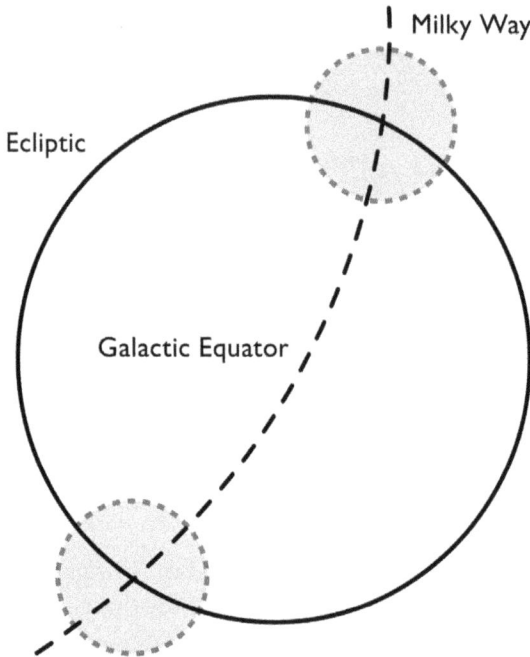

Figure 4: the cross formed by the intersection of the Milky Way and the ecliptic

With the naked eye, we can see the bulge at the center of the Milky Way and a dark rift, which marks our galactic center. We now know through recent scientific investigations that this dark area is the black hole at the center of our galaxy. Many ancient cultures seemed to have understood in their own ways that this dark void marked the source of the life in the galaxy and on Earth. In this way, the human womb was seen as a mirror of the cosmic "womb." "As above, so below." As the creative birth-giving ability of women was honored on Earth, so it was also reflected in the sky, with the vagina of the goddess residing at the center of our universe, giving birth to the stars and planets of the galaxy and all of life. Is it any wonder then that the yoni, the image and symbol of the vagina is the earliest and most sacred symbol? We see this symbol appearing over and over again on the early goddess images found all over the world. The Milky Way was viewed both as the source of life and as the place that souls returned to at the time of death. As the source and World Tree, it not only held the Earth and sky together but also weaved together the realms of life and death, of the visible world and the invisible realms.

The constellation Cygnus (seen as a vulture, bird, or swan in most cultures across time) is in alignment with the part of the Milky Way where the galactic center resides. In his recent book *The Cygnus Mystery: Unlocking the Ancient Secret of Life's Origins in the Cosmos*, researcher Andrew Collins noted that the oldest known temple, Gobekli Tepe (meaning "hill of the navel"), built around 9500 BCE in what is now the land between Syria and Iraq, was in exact alignment with this constellation. He speculated that this temple may have hearkened back to earlier cults honoring the time when Cygnus' brightest star, Deneb, was the celestial pole (dating back seventeen thousand years). If this speculation is true, then our ancient ancestors were in tune with these critical markers in the sky for thousands of years. It is interesting to note that the stars of Cygnus also form a cross, reflecting the symbol throughout the ages for the medicine wheel and the World Tree, which both honor the source and four directions that hold all life intact.

With the cross of the line of the ecliptic and the Milky Way, the path of the Milky Way was often seen as the north/south axis while the ecliptic formed the east/west axis of a cross. As was noted before, this concept is reflective of the ancient mandala or medicine wheel found in all ancient and current indigenous cultures in which the people orient their outer (and inner) worlds in accordance with the four directions and the wheel of life. Ancient cultures often organized their villages in replication of this pattern, locating the center of their region and honoring it as the place of power and of the most sacred sites (for standing stones or temples) with the larger area then bounded by landmarks signifying the four directions.

For example, ancient Ireland was divided into four quarters around a central point long before the Celts arrived (twenty-five hundred years ago). This fivefold structure (four cardinal points and the center) was reflected in Irish gold discs as well as in their mythology and in Irish sayings such as "into the five points" and "the five parts of the world," meaning in all directions (see Dames, Michael, *Mythic Ireland*, pp. 15-

16). In ancient Egypt, the pyramids of Giza and other critical sacred sites were built in alignment with the celestial meridian, tracing a line from south to north and dividing the sky into east and west. Also, the Egyptian pharaohs, each year at an annual renewal ceremony would raise the djed, or sacred pole, associated with stability and the backbone of the deity Osiris and reminiscent of the cross of the World Tree.

At times, the Milky Way was also viewed as a serpent. For example, the ancient Mayans referred to the winter Milky Way as the "white boned serpent." They also viewed their bird deity, Itzam Ye, as residing at the top of the World Tree. Perhaps this combination of images is what led to the deity Quetzalcoatl, the sacred winged serpent. Perhaps this winged serpent is related to the constellation of Cygnus, the bird, in its prominent placement with the Milky Way, the serpent. References to a bird and serpent in the World Tree can also be found in the Sumerian creation myth. We also see the centrality of the serpent in the biblical Genesis story. In archeology, the most ancient goddess images are of the bird and serpent goddess figures dating back to approximately 30,000 BCE. It is noteworthy to consider how this integration of the bird and the serpent portrays the unity and integration of the Earth and the sky.

Of particular significance to many of these ancient cultures was when one of the equinox or solstice points of the ecliptic aligned with the galactic center, the black hole at the center of our galaxy. The Milky Way extends from Sagittarius to Gemini in our zodiac with the galactic center located near three degrees of Sagittarius in the sidereal zodiac and at twenty-six degrees of Sagittarius in the tropical zodiac. Throughout many cultures, the constellation of Sagittarius was seen as a bow and arrow or an archer with the tip of the arrow pointed toward the galactic center. On the other side of the galactic center are the constellations Ophiuchus (the Serpent Bearer) and Scorpius (correlating with the sign, Scorpio). In many myths, we see references to the entryway to immortality being guarded by the "scorpion men" (for example in the Mesopotamian epic of Gilgamesh). Perhaps this is also the source of the ancient association of Scorpio with death and rebirth.

We find in ancient cultures a sophisticated understanding of astronomy, of the path of the Sun and planets, and of the critical solstice and equinox points. They also showed an awareness of the precession of the equinoxes. As the planets and stars moved above them, the point of stillness, the celestial polar point, also became a sacred center. The World Tree was seen as extending from the Earth and rooted in this still point in the sky.

For many thousands of years prior to 4500 BCE (near the beginning of the Age of Taurus), there was no polestar. The still point around which the other stars circled was in darkness. From 4500 to 2000 BCE, Draco's stars were the polestars with Thuban as the focal point as the brightest star and closest to the celestial pole (Brady, p. 134). As Brady notes, throughout the ages, Draco was seen as a "snake, a dragon or a serpent" (Brady, p. 134). In the earliest times, this dragon image incorporated what we now know as Ursa Major and Ursa Minor and was seen as half bird and half snake (Brady, p. 134). This again correlates with the earliest known goddess images, which were the bird and serpent goddesses dating back as early as Upper Paleolithic cultures.

For these early prehistoric cultures, it is likely that the dark stillness at the center of the sky (near the polestar as well as at the galactic center) was seen as the origin of life, the fecund void from which we come and to which we return at death, much like the earthly caves were honored as womb and tomb. The color black was the color of life and fertility, correlating with the black fertile soil as well as the black center of the sky. For these cultures, the night was sacred and the Moon was honored as the primary sky deity, more than the Sun. The ancient image of the triple goddess arose from the Moon in her phases as crescent, full and waning or dark Moon. From 33,000 BCE on, we find archeological evidence of bones marking the lunar phases and carvings correlating the Moon with the life cycle of plants and with women's menstruation and ovulation.

During the Age of Gemini, when the Sun was rising at the time of the vernal equinox behind the constellation Gemini, the Sun and Milky Way were in alignment with each other. This period has been referred to as the "Golden Age," and there is some speculation that as the vernal equinox Sun's rising and Milky Way separated, this led to the creation myths about being expelled from paradise, such as the Genesis story of Adam and Eve being expelled from the Garden of Eden. Adam and Eve were sent away because they had eaten from the Tree of Knowledge and were now self-conscious, knowing their separateness from the Divine. Perhaps, ancient cultures were sobered by the realization that our world can in fact move out of alignment with the Milky Way and separate from our source. Yet we move away only to come back into connection. The understanding of the dialectic of separation and return became a living reality seen in the sky. Ancient cultures noted these larger epochs of time and the movement of the stars in the precessional cycle. Currently, since AD 1998, the Sun at the time of the winter solstice has been in alignment with the galactic center (in Sagittarius) and will continue to be within orb for several more years (see Figure 5 below). In ancient times, this was thought to be a time of profound connection with the source of all life and a time when our consciousness is able to come more fully into alignment with the creative intelligence of the universe.

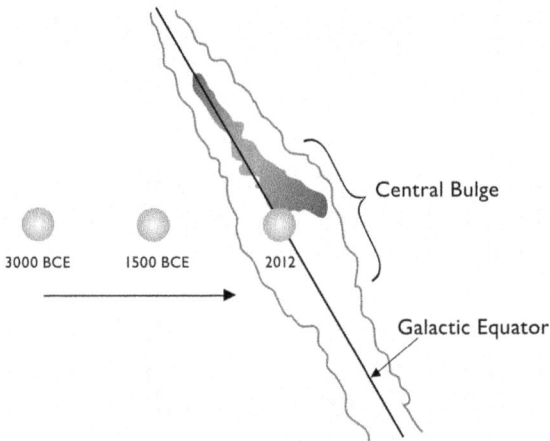

Figure 5: Image of Sun/Milky Way alignment – courtesy of andrewcollins.com

PART TWO

EXPLORING THE ARCHETYPAL THEMES OF THE AGES

INTRODUCTION

In exploring the archetypal themes and patterns of the ages prior to our historical period, we need to rely on the archeological record and what we know of those periods of human and cultural development. We also need to be aware that, while the archetypal patterns are analogous to energy fields that exist around us in the universe mirrored in the cycles of the stars and planets, our interpretations of them are also shaped by our cultural and psychological perceptions. These summaries of the ages then are not a definitive explanation but rather an exploration of some of the correlations between our understanding of the archetypal themes and the cultural patterns of the times.

It is also important to note that the development of the twelve signs of the zodiac as we know them dates from approximately AD 630 (see Robert Hand's article, "The History of Astrology: Another View"). The earliest astrological records known date from ancient Mesopotamia (around 2300 BCE) and are the omen and divination lore of "Enuma Anu Enlil" recording the movements of the stars and planets and their meanings for the life of the community. The earliest Babylonian records indicate that the original zodiac consisted of six signs (not twelve), each consisting of sixty degrees rather than the traditional thirty degrees. The constellation of Taurus, or the Bull, was much larger than our current configuration. The current signs of Pisces and Aquarius were seen as the Babylonian "Fish-Man," while Capricorn was seen as the "Goat-Fish." The stars of Libra were incorporated into the sign of Scorpio and were seen as the claws of the scorpion. The zodiac as we now know it developed later and was originally used for locating the position of the Sun through the cycle of the year.

It is significant to note that across history, our conceptions of the sky have moved from a more holistic and integrated tapestry to an increasingly fragmented compilation of images. This change reflects the shift from the right-brain dominance of prehistoric cultures to the left-brain analytical way of knowing of the historical era. It also reflects our increasing sense of separation and fragmentation culturally.

As we review the precession of the equinoxes and the past astrological ages, we will use the lens of our current zodiac to see how these themes manifested in those times. We will also explore how the themes of each sign incorporate the meaning of the polarity sign in the wheel of the zodiac as the sub-age, or second half of the precessional age. Jeffrey Wolf Green has proposed this format as a way of understanding the shifting themes during these astrological periods (see Green, "Astrological Ages and Sub-Ages," evolutionaryastrology.net). For example, he conjectured that the latter half of the age (or second sub-age) reflects the energy and archetypes of the opposing sign of the zodiac and is an effort of the collective consciousness to come to a more balanced integration of the meaning of each sign. We will also weave into our understanding of the signs of the zodiac the planets that are associated with them (as the rulers of the signs), dating from classical Greek culture to the present. Determinations of the exact beginning and ending dates of each age vary to some degree among astrologers. What are important are the themes of the larger time periods and not the exact dates, since these can not be determined in any definitive way. For this exploration of the ages, we will use the dates proposed by astrologer Jeffrey Wolf Green.

CHAPTER FOUR

THE AGE OF LEO (10,900-8,740 BCE)

This period of time in prehistory marks the transition from the Paleolithic Age (Old Stone Age) to the Mesolithic (Middle Stone) Age. During this time, people began to domesticate animals and move toward settlements and away from the hunter-gatherer way of life.

The constellation Leo has been perceived by cultures across time as a lion figure. This image was associated with these stars in ancient Babylon, Egypt, Persia, Syria and then later by the Turks and Jews (Brady, *Brady's Book of Fixed Stars,* p. 259). There is increasing evidence that the Sphinx (the half-human and half-lion figure) in Egypt was built during this period (approximately 10,500 BCE or earlier, see Hancock, *Fingerprints of the Gods,* p. 423) facing due east at the time when the constellation Leo was rising at the spring equinox.

This is also the age when the earliest pyramids were constructed in Mexico and Egypt. While the conventional view of archeologists is that the Great Pyramids in Egypt were constructed about 2700-2500 BCE, Graham Hancock and Robert Bauval cite recent research (particularly from the field of archeoastronomy) positing that some of the pyramids were built much earlier, during the Age of Leo (see Hancock and Bauval, *The Message of the Sphinx: A Quest for the Hidden Legacy of Mankind*). The Great Pyramids in Egypt were positioned in a formation patterned after the stars of Orion's belt as they appeared in the sky at the cusp of this age (see Bauval and Gilbert, *The Orion Mystery*). These three stars of Orion were at their lowest point in the sky at the time when Leo rose on the horizon at the time of the spring equinox in about

10,500 BCE (Hancock and Bauval, *The Message of the Sphinx: A Quest for the Hidden Legacy of Mankind*, p. 81). However, if we use the later traditional dating of the Great Pyramids of around 2450 BCE, we find that the pyramids would have been built in a precise alignment with Polaris (the polestar) as well as critical configurations with Orion and the bright stars of Auriga (see Vidler, *The Star Mirror*, pp. 58-63).

Interestingly, an alternative view of the star alignments of the Great Pyramids of Giza has recently been proposed by Andrew Collins in his book *The Cygnus Mystery: Unlocking the Ancient Secret of Life's Origins in the Cosmos* (2007). He suggests that the pyramids were built in alignment with the primary stars of the Cygnus constellation, and that this reflects the ancient Egyptians' honoring of this bird-god, or in their cosmology, the falcon-headed god, who guides souls to the path of the Milky Way after death. As was described before, this constellation marks the dark rift at the northern end of the Milky Way and was seen by many cultures as the mediator, leading souls to and from source, our galactic center. This constellation may also have been critical in the ancient Egyptians' mapping of the meridian line to the celestial pole.

Whatever the exact star configurations used, the precision of the architecture of the pyramids and their alignments to specific stars is beyond question. The pyramids were built in precise alignment with stars to bring the land and rulers into right relationship with the energies of the stars and of the universe, and they were viewed not only as burial sites but also as places of initiation into the realm of the Divine (the starry sky). The souls of those who died were thought to become one with the star deities. In our modern era, we continue to be baffled by the sophistication of the technological and astronomical understanding of this ancient culture. We are still unable to decipher the way in which the pyramids were built with such precision and accuracy.

For the Egyptians, the constellation Orion was extremely important and was the celestial counterpart of their deity, Osiris, and it was known as "Sah", the "Far-Strider" (Hancock and Bauval, *The Message of the Sphinx: A Quest for the Hidden Legacy of Mankind*, p. 81). In ancient Egypt, Orion's rising, later incorporated into the myths of Osiris, was an important calendrical and spiritual marker in their culture across thousands of years. Osiris was the god of vegetation and was symbolic of the fertility of the land. In Egyptian mythology dating back at least to 4000 BCE, Osiris was slain by his jealous brother, Set, and then revived by Isis, his sister and wife and the great goddess and mother of all of life.

The constellation of Orion, symbolizing Osiris rose in ancient Egypt before the rising of the star, Sirius (Isis), and at the time of the summer flooding of the Nile bringing life-giving water to the desert. In ancient Egypt, being in alignment, in right relationship with the stars was a critical part of their cosmology. The pharaohs believed that after death they traveled to Osiris (Orion) to be reborn as a star (Vidler, *The Star Mirror,* p. 62).

Part of the annual ritual to honor the Egyptian New Year and Osiris' resurrection was the raising of the djed. Djed means "to be stable, to be firmly established," and this annual ritual was a way to come back into alignment with the energies of the Earth and sky and to ensure that the pharaoh was in right relationship with Maat, the energies of the universe. Perhaps these later myths and rituals hearken back to earlier practices dating from the Age of Leo.

Geological evidence indicates that the erosion patterns on the Sphinx fit with the weather conditions in 10,500 BCE at the beginning of the Age of Leo (see Hancock and Bauval, *The Message of the Sphinx: A Quest for the Hidden Legacy of Mankind,* p. 17). The nature of the erosion fits with rain damage rather than being from wind or sand. This finding places the dating of the Sphinx at approximately 7000-5000 BCE or earlier due to the changes in the weather patterns after that period (i.e., desertification) (Hancock and Bauval, pp. 19-20). The Sphinx was often referred to by the ancient Egyptians as "Seshep-ankh Atum," "the living image of Atum," who was the Sun god and original deity of their pantheon (Hancock and Bauval, p. 5). Our word "Sphinx" is a corruption (through Greek) of this name (Hancock and Bauval, p. 5). When the Sun was rising with the constellation Leo on the eastern horizon at the spring equinox, the Sphinx was likely built to face east toward the stars of Leo, and the pyramids were in the exact configuration of Orion's belt in the sky at that time (Hancock and Bauval, p. 77). "As above, so below."

It is clear that the ancient Egyptians were gifted astronomers in that they have constructed the sides of the pyramids to face exactly the cardinal directions (north, south, east, and west) within threesixtieths of a degree of error (Hancock and Bauval, pp. 61-62). While this earlier dating of the Sphinx (and possibly of the Great Pyramids) is uncertain, it is increasingly supported by the evidence of the field of archeoastronomy.

Also, during this age, 9000 BCE marked the recession of the most recent ice age, allowing an increase in the expansion of human populations. With this climatic change and the melting of the ice came a period of floods. The current landmasses that constitute our continents only began to take their current forms in the period between 15,000 and 5,000 BCE (Hancock, *Underworld,* p. 53). It must be noted that floods are memorialized in the mythology of most ancient cultures. The periods of most cataclysmic flooding caused by the melting ice occurred in three periods: around 13,000-12000 BCE, 10,000-8000 BCE and then 6000-4000 BCE. Accompanying the mass flooding were dramatic Earth changes, including earthquakes and volcanic eruptions (see Hancock, *Underworld,* pp. 65-69).

In *Underworld: The Mysterious Origins of Civilization,* Graham Hancock cites recent research indicating that these massive floods destroyed some of the oldest and most ancient civilizations located in the coastal regions that now are beneath the surface of the sea. Current undersea archeological explorations are discovering ruins of ancient cities off the coasts of India, Malta, Japan, and China, among other regions. These recent discoveries raise profound questions. What if our modern civilizations are the outgrowth of the survivors of these ancient cataclysmic floods? Could it be, as the Hindus suggest in their view of the ages of human development, that much of our historical period is actually an Age of Ignorance (the Kali Yuga, when we have lost awareness of the wisdom that we once knew) rather than the pinnacle of human development as we like to imagine? This concept might help explain the disjuncture between the more advanced ancient cultures such as the one in ancient Egypt and the other Neolithic cultures. Perhaps remnants of these advanced civilizations from the coastal regions survived and seeded the sites of ancient cultures such as that of ancient Egypt while the surrounding cultures were far less advanced.

Interestingly, later in ancient Egypt, when the constellation Leo was rising at the time of the summer solstice (approximately 6000 to 3000 BCE), these stars were associated with the flooding of the

Nile (Brady, *Brady's Book of Fixed Stars*, p. 259). Thus Leo came to represent the deity protecting the sacred waters of life, fertilizing the dry land. In this way, we frequently see, in ancient and modern times, lion's-head sculptures on fountains, symbolizing the lion's role in protecting the flowing water. This observation also brings us to an interesting correlation between the constellation of Leo and its polarity constellation, Aquarius, which has been viewed in most cultures as the water-bearer or the urn bringing the life-giving water to the Earth.

The archetypal themes of Aquarius color the second half of the Age of Leo. In this sub-age, we see an increasing expansion and development of social culture associated with the archetypal themes of Aquarius. This sign's traditional astrological planetary ruler is Saturn. Saturn is about form and structure and, in ruling Aquarius, provides the capacity to manifest the creative impulses of Leo in concrete form. This interpretation is certainly evident in the construction of some of the ancient monuments of this period, as well as in the development of human settlements across the Middle East and Old Europe.

This later association of the constellation Leo with the summer solstice may also relate to the connection since that time of Leo with the heat and light of summer. Our current associations of Leo with the lion date from this period in that it is toward the end of this period that writing originated, allowing us to begin to connect with the mythology of the time (see Brady, p. 259). Bernadette Brady notes that the earliest known mythological use of the lion was the Egyptian lion goddess, Sekhmet (p. 259). Sekhmet used fire to scorch and consume her father's enemies, reflecting the association of Leo to the fierce light and heat of the Sun during the longest days of the summer. According to Brady, "at all times in Egyptian mythology the lion is linked to a goddess, aggressive, assertive, known by many titles and names, the 'Lady of Flame' or 'great lady, holy one, powerful one,' for example" (Brady, p. 259).

In traditional astrology, the sign Leo is known as a fixed fire sign associated with the inspiration and fire of spirit manifesting in creativity. It is associated with the heart in medical astrology. At the heart of the lion in the constellation is the star Regulus. This star is one of the royal stars of Persia and the guardian of the North. Historically, it has been associated with leadership and with the importance of ruling from the heart rather than seeking power or success through revenge.

The traditional astrological ruler of the sign Leo is the Sun, our star. It is interesting that many of the hieroglyphic images from ancient Egypt show the orb of the Sun over the head; for example, in the images of Isis. Also, many ancient cultures dating back to the Age of Leo, such as those of the pre-Incan sites in Peru, seem to reflect an understanding of ways in which the life-giving energy of the Sun could be harnessed not only for harvesting the land but also for increasing human health and consciousness. Interestingly, in our times, Hira Ratan Manek has discovered an ancient Hindu ritual of Sun-gazing that significantly enhances the functioning of the pineal gland and allows a person to use the Sun's energy for nutrition, healing and increased consciousness and well-being.

Hira Ratan Manek has been studied by many medical centers around the world and has been able to use solar energy to provide his nutrition, fasting from food for prolonged periods of time while thriving through the integration of the energy from the Sun. Hira Ratan Manek contends that the Sun's energy has benefits for us physically, mentally, and spiritually that have been forgotten in modern times. He has now established the Solar Healing Center in Florida to continue to conduct research on this ancient practice.

In integrating the wisdom of the Age of Leo, perhaps we can remember and begin to work again with the power and healing effects of the Sun. This age also reminds us of the wisdom of the lion, of living in courage from the heart and of finding our power through being in right relationship with all of life, rather than seeking the illusion of power through manipulation and revenge.

CHAPTER FIVE

THE AGE OF CANCER (8740-6580 BCE)

In this period, Cancer was rising at the time of the vernal equinox. During this time, agricultural communities began to develop. Some of the earliest settlements (in Catal Huyuk, 6500 BCE and southeastern Europe, 7000 BCE) date from this time. It is the time of the "Fertile Crescent" cultures that were established on the banks of the Nile in Egypt, on the Tigris and Euphrates Rivers in Mesopotamia, and on the Indus River in India. Ruins from these sites show the predominance of worship of the goddess, with the architecture of the settlements built in feminine shapes (George, *Mysteries of the Dark Moon: The Healing Power of the Goddess*, p. 87). The Neolithic people had a strong association of the Earth as a fertile mother giving birth to plants, and the grain goddess was a dominant deity in the cultures of Old Europe. With Cancer rising at the time of spring, these stars may have been associated with the life-giving Earth mother.

Since the time of classical Greece, Cancer has been associated with the water element. It is noteworthy that during the Age of Cancer, images of goddesses with breasts marked by Vs and chevrons were prevalent in Old Europe. Archeologist Maria Gimbutas indicates that breasts marked with these lines symbolize "the Bird Goddess as the Divine Source of Nourishment, milk/rain, or as the Giver of Life in general" (Gimbutas, *The Language of the Goddess*, p. 31). According to Gimbutas, in the iconography of prehistoric times throughout the world, water was depicted as in the "zig-zag" or "serpentine" image (Gimbutas, p. 19). The "M sign" is an abbreviated zig-zag.

"In Magdaleian times (approx. 15,000-9,000 BCE) and later in Old Europe, zig-zags and Ms are found engraved or painted within uterine and lens (vulva) shapes, suggesting the symbolic affinity between the zig-zag, M, female moisture, and amniotic fluid" (Gimbutas, p. 19). The M sign is later seen in the Egyptian hieroglyph M, "mu," meaning water, and in the ancient Greek letter M, "mu" (Gimbutas, p. 19).

In the historical era, Cancer was first linked with the image of the crab by the Chaldeans due to the Sun's apparent sideways movement through this constellation (see Brady, *Brady's Book of Fixed Stars*, p. 253). In a later period, about 2000 BCE (at the beginning of the Age of Aries), Cancer was positioned to rise at the time of the summer solstice. In ancient Egypt, in this period, Cancer was seen as the scarab beetle, which was a symbol of immortality, the place where the Sun god was reborn (Brady, p. 253). Later, the belief developed in ancient Egypt that this was the place where human souls entered into the Earth's material realms, the place of the soul's incarnation, while the stars of Capricorn (rising at the winter solstice) were seen as the place of the soul's departure at death (Brady, p. 253). For the Egyptians, the scarab beetle was associated with the third form of the Sun god Ra, "Khepera," who in their creation myths was the force rising from the primeval water and was the source of all life (Brady, p. 254).

In traditional astrology, the sign Cancer is known as a cardinal water sign, and in medical astrology it is associated with breasts and with the womb. Again, there is a strong association of Cancer throughout mythology with the Great Goddess and the source of all life. The traditional astrological ruler of this sign is the Moon, which makes sense given the strong link between the Moon and the sacred feminine.

In more recent times, Cancer has been the constellation rising at the time of the summer solstice, so it may seem strange that the constellation is correlated with the Moon and not the Sun. Guttman and Johnson attribute this to the fact that at the time of the summer solstice, the Sun is turning back and moving back into the darkness (Guttman and Johnson, *Mythic Astrology*, p. 265). However, the symbolism of the Moon with Cancer may trace back to the earlier era when Cancer rose at the time of the vernal equinox and the agricultural communities were wedded to the cycles of the Moon and the correlations between the Moon and planting.

Until the patriarchal period, the calendar was a lunar calendar and the night was seen as more sacred than day, and the Moon was associated with the ancient goddess traditions. Engraved bones dating back to 25,000 BCE (see Marshack, *The Roots of Civilization*, p. 48, cited in Cashford, *The Moon: Myth and Image*, p. 17) show the observations and notations of the phases of the Moon. The goddess of Laussel from Dordogne, France (circa 22,000-18,000 BCE) clearly demonstrates the early associations between the lunar phases and women's fertility. In this way, from the Upper Paleolithic period on, we see the intimate relationship between the Moon and the life-giving womb of women. For thousands of years, caves, representative of the womb, were sites of sacred ceremony and of honoring the goddess.

The Moon in ancient cultures was also linked with the rain and life-giving waters. Cashford writes, in *The Moon: Myth and Image*, that:

> When the thin curve of the Crescent Moon rose as new out of the black night, it appeared to many people to be a cup which held all the waters of life: rain, dew, the moisture of air and cloud, the water of springs, rivers, seas, the sap of plants and trees, and the blood and milk of animals and human beings.
>
> (Cashford, p. 68)

As was stated above, the Moon has also been deeply associated with women's fertility and procreative power for over twenty-five thousand years. The origin of the triple goddess (dating back to Paleolithic times) comes from the waxing, full, and waning phases of the Moon. These in turn are related to the phases of women's lives as "maiden," "mother," and "crone." For women in ancient times, living in close relationship with the Earth and sky, the pineal gland affected by the moonlight caused women's menstrual cycles to be in relationship with the phases of the Moon. Women would ovulate at the time of the full Moon and menstruate at the time of the dark Moon. For many ancient cultures (and currently among many indigenous cultures), women retreated together at the time of the dark Moon to menstruate, meditate, and bring back visions for the community. The time of the dark Moon was the time of deep transformation, of death and rebirth. It was also the time when the Sun was conjunct the Moon, the time of the sacred marriage of solar and lunar energy.

Related to this, the dark Moon was also the time in many ancient cultures in which the sacred sexual ceremonies took place. Women's sexuality was understood as bipolar in nature, with periods of intense sexual energy at both the times of ovulation and of menstruation. The time of ovulation related to the life-giving, birthing force of sexuality resulting in childbearing. The time of bleeding was a time of deep power and healing, of connection with the energies of life, death, and rebirth. To engage in the sexual act at this time was to encounter the power of the life-giving and death-bringing goddess.

We see evidence of this idea in many ancient myths. For example, the first known written myth from Sumer describes Lilith who was the handmaiden of Inanna (child of the Moon god) who brought the men from the fields to the sacred temple for the sexual rites at the time of the dark Moon. In later times, this myth changed as Lilith began to represent the image of a "harlot," a destructive seductress who came at night to torment men and endanger infants and pregnant women. In Hebrew mythology, Lilith was seen as the first wife of Adam and was banished for refusing to submit to his dominance. A view of sexuality as "ungodly" pervades ancient Hebrew legends about Lilith, and she is replaced by the more accommodating Eve (Baring and Cashford, *The Myth of the Goddess: Evolution of an Image*, p. 512). Over time, Lilith became associated with women's sexuality as dangerous or evil, and darkness with punishment and death rather than darkness as an entrance to the transformative power of the goddess.

As the shift into patriarchy occurred, this free and independent expression of women's power and sexuality became seen as a threat and had to be subverted and repressed. "In both orthodox and apocryphal literature, Lilith's shadow falls on women as far forward in time as the fifteenth century A.D., when in the same imagery as was employed for Lilith, thousands were accused of copulating with demons, killing infants and seducing men, of being ... witches," (Cashford and Baring, p. 512). During the burning times in Europe (approximately AD 1300-1700), many of the women accused of being witches were in fact called "liliths."

This weaving of the power and healing nature of women's sexuality (separate from procreation) was also apparent in the early mythology of Medusa. The name "Medusa" comes from the Sanskrit word "Medha," meaning "sovereign female wisdom." She was associated with the dark of the Moon, and she was worshipped as a primary goddess in ancient Egypt and by the Libyan Amazons in North Africa, and she was later incorporated into Cretan and Greek mythology. The origin of the gorgon masks was that these were worn by women during sacred ceremonies, such as the sexual rites, to indicate their deep connection with the goddess and as a form of protection.

The goddess Medusa was also very connected with the power of the menstrual blood. In the later Greek version, her blood was given to the healer Asklepios, and it had the power to heal or to destroy. Interestingly, the blood from the right side of her body (associated with the movement of the waxing Moon) was healing, while the blood from her left side (symbolic of the waning Moon) had the power to kill. While in earlier times, the menstrual blood and the sacred sexual rites were about the life/death transformative nature of the goddess and a deep connection with her, in the patriarchal period, they become associated primarily with death, with "uncleanness," and with destruction. In Greek mythology, Medusa's stare turns men to stone. In Hebrew beliefs and practices, menstruating women were "unclean" and must be kept apart from the community. The power of women's menstrual blood and of these early sacred sexual ceremonies, which were originally about the healing and merging with the energy of the goddess, became denigrated into agents of death and destruction. During the patriarchal period, as male dominance became the cultural norm, it was necessary to undermine and repress this deep power of the female body and of women's sexuality.

In the Age of Cancer, when the Moon was honored, sexuality and women's bodies were viewed as sacred, as symbolic of the creativity and fertility of the goddess. There was a deep understanding of the life-giving nature of women's menstrual blood, mothers' milk and the waters of the Earth. All of life was a part of the "Great Round." Death was not to be feared but was only one aspect of a larger cycle. As the waning Moon gave birth to the new Moon, so the tomb was also the womb, death emerging in new life. The aspects of the goddess as life-giver and death-bringer were not split but were part of a unified whole.

The sub-age of Cancer is Capricorn (the sign opposite Cancer), and it is traditionally ruled by Saturn. This sign of the zodiac relates to the development of structure and culture. In ancient Babylon and in many ancient cultures, this constellation was seen as the "goat-fish" or the goat with a fish's tail. This sea-goat in Babylonian mythology was the god Ea or "He of Vast Intellect." Ea was the protector of his people and the one who brought the people the wisdom of agriculture and of how to live in community. This sign signified the wise teachers who were thought to come from the sea in the form of a fish and to change into the form of a goat to move on the land and teach the people, only to then return once again to the sea. Arising from the waters of Cancer, the energy of Capricorn brought the awareness of how to manifest visions in action and how to live in tangible ways on the Earth and in community.

As we reintegrate the meaning and wisdom of the Age of Cancer, we are able to reconnect with the lineage of the sacred feminine and the meaning of the life/death/rebirth cycle of the Moon. In so doing, we are able to correct the imbalances of the patriarchal period and come back into right relationship with our bodies and with the natural world around us. Our understanding of spirit and matter, of male and female, of light and dark, no longer needs to be polarized. With the energy of Capricorn, we are able to integrate this embodied wisdom and manifest it in our daily lives.

CHAPTER SIX

THE AGE OF GEMINI (6580-4420 BCE)

In traditional astrology, Gemini is a mutable air sign and is associated with the planet Mercury. Mercury is a small planet that never moves more than twenty-eight degrees from the Sun, and across cultures it has been seen as a messenger. Mercury and the sign Gemini are symbolic of mental activity, learning, and teaching and a hunger for knowledge. It is during this age that we see the first experiments in writing, which then emerged more fully in the Age of Taurus.

The sub-age of Gemini is Sagittarius. Since ancient times, this constellation has been seen as an image of an archer or of a bow and arrow. In later ages, this sign was associated with the energy of war and the rise of archers who were lethal in that they could kill from afar. However, in more ancient times, it was likely known that the tip of the arrow of the archer pointed toward the rift in the Milky Way and the galactic center. In its deeper archetypal meaning, Sagittarius speaks to our quest for source, for the deeper meaning of life. As Gemini helps us to learn and gather knowledge, Sagittarius guides us in understanding the broader meaning and purpose of this knowledge. Together, Gemini and Sagittarius integrate knowledge and wisdom, and it is significant that both of the constellations lie near the path of the Milky Way, from ancient times seen as the source of incarnation and of life.

The Age of Gemini, during the later part of the Neolithic era, was characterized by an increasing settlement of communities focused on food production, as well as the development of domestication of animals and increased production of pottery and weaving. Stone tools were also widely utilized. All of these activities involve community interaction and learning, which are characteristics of the Gemini archetype.

In most ancient cultures - including the ancient Egyptians, Hebrews, and Celts - the two companion stars of Gemini (Castor and Pollux) and the rest of the constellation were seen as the image of two figures, or twins. In later Greek culture, the two stars were associated with the light and the dark. This was the case in other cultures as well. For example, in later Egyptian beliefs, these stars were seen as the struggle between Horus (god of the morning star) and Set (god of the evening star) (Brady, *Brady's Book of Fixed Stars*, p. 243). The twins thus became associated with the notion of polarity and with the struggle between good and evil or light and dark.

However, these were later beliefs attached to the twins. In more ancient times, when these stars rose at the time of the vernal equinox, images of the twin goddesses emerged in Old Europe. In the *The Language of the Goddess*, Maria Gimbutas reported that "double-headed goddesses" or mother-daughter images appeared throughout the Neolithic and Copper Ages and were found in Catal Huyuk (circa 6500 BCE), as well as at the site of the Vinca culture. She noted that the heads of these figures often showed attributes of the bird goddess, with heads that were beaked and with bodies covered with chevrons, meanders, and crossbands (see p. 171). These female double goddesses at times depicted two adults (perhaps sisters) and, at other times, seemed to be the image of a mother and child.

In her book *The Double Goddess: Women Sharing Power*, Vicki Noble explored the possible cultural meanings of the twin goddesses that have been found in ancient cultures extending from the Middle East to central Asia, India, Tibet, Mexico, and Peru. She posited that these images across time and cultures may have represented the multifaceted archetypal patterns of women's relationships, including those of mother/daughter and female collaborative leadership, as well as of lovers. She also associated these twin goddesses with the dual nature of the great goddess in her lunar and solar aspects, as well as in her being the creatrix and destroyer, bringer of life and death.

As was stated previously, it was also during this age that the path of the ecliptic coincided with the Milky Way. At the end of this age, the movement of the Sun and planets in the sky began to separate from the Milky Way, and this movement may have been the impetus for the creation myths arising from the end of this age which refer to being cast out from Paradise. Throughout many ancient cultures, the Milky Way was seen as the path of the sacred and the source of life or the place of immortality. With the separation of the ecliptic from this path, the world of humanity was separated from the path of the Divine. As in the Garden of Eden myth in the Old Testament of the Bible, Adam and Eve become conscious of their identity as separate from God and were thrust out of the garden. This myth may relate to some of the later beliefs associating the twin stars with the theme of polarity and how they are often depicted as exemplifying the struggle between good and evil or light and dark.

Could the Age of Gemini have been a period when the first seeds of human duality consciousness, of self and other and of polarization, began? This also may be the time in which we began to have a sense of the separation between Earth and sky. For the time prior to that, there is evidence that the cosmos was experienced as a unified whole. In fact, in ancient Sumer, the term for the world was "heaven-earth," the sphere above and beneath as the realm within which we reside.

Another important possible association with Gemini and the twin stars Castor and Pollux may be found in the creation story of the ancient Mayans in the Popol Vuh (written and translated in the 1500s but dating back in oral tradition to a much earlier time). In his books *Maya Cosmogenesis 2012* (with Terrence McKenna) and *Galactic Alignment: The Transformation of Consciousness According to the Mayan, Egyptian and Vedic Traditions*, John Major Jenkins has done pioneering research as to the astronomical configurations referenced in the Popol Vuh and in the Mayan long-count calendar and the monuments at Izapa, Mexico, the central site for the classical Mayan civilization and the place where the long-count calendar was created. The ancient Mayan long-count calendar tracks the current world age from a start date of August 11, 3114 BCE to an end date on the winter solstice, December 21, 2012. On this winter solstice date, the Sun will rise in conjunction with the galactic center and mark the end of the twenty-six-thousand-year precessional cycle.

Jenkins examines the creation story of the Popol Vuh and shows how it is related to these astronomical events. He describes how the solar lord, Hunahpu, in the story is resurrected at this date. Previously, Hunahpu had been defeated and killed by the lords of the underworld, Xibalba (the dark rift at the galactic center). His sons, the Hero Twins, rescue him after journeying to Xibalba, the lower world, and avenging their father. In the process, the Hero Twins also defeat the deity of the previous age, Seven Macaw, who then falls from the sky. Jenkins equates Seven Macaw with the stars of the Big Dipper (Ursa Major) and contends that the myth is describing the shift in Mayan cosmology from a focus on the celestial pole (guarded by Ursa Major) to a focus on the galactic center as the primary source and deity.

If we add to Jenkins' astronomical associations, we might see the Hero Twins as the twin stars of Gemini, Castor and Pollux, who throughout time and across cultures have been seen as sacred twins in world mythology. Toward the end of the Age of Gemini, when the stars of Gemini still rose with the Sun at the time of the vernal equinox, Thuban became the celestial polestar and was in this location from approximately 4500 BCE to 2000 BCE (see Brady, *Brady's Book of Stars*, p. 133). The stars of the Big Dipper, Seven Macaw, circled around the celestial pole, marking this sacred portal. However, around 2000 BCE, the celestial pole began to shift away from Thuban toward Polaris, our current celestial polestar. At about the same time, the stars of Gemini had sunk below the horizon, no longer rising before the Sun at the vernal equinox, and were now replaced by the stars of Taurus. Polaris is at the tip of the constellation Ursa Minor and is much further from the stars of the Big Dipper. Perhaps this is the meaning of the fall of the Seven Macaw. As the Hero Twins, the stars of Gemini, descended into the lower world, they engaged with the lords of the underworld and with the Seven Macaw and eventually helped to revive their father. It must also be noted that the Sun aligns with the Milky Way only within the constellations of Scorpio and Sagittarius near the galactic center and with the stars of Taurus and Gemini at the other end of the sky. In this way, we can see how the Hero Twins, opposite the stars of Sagittarius, can easily be seen as the offspring of their father, the solar lord, winter solstice Sun in Sagittarius.

Of significance in this story and in the archetypal meaning of the sign of Gemini is the understanding of our profound relationship with the galactic center. As was anticipated in the Mayan long-count calendar, we are now in a critical time period when our winter solstice Sun is in alignment with the galactic center, marking the end of a twenty-six-thousand-year cycle (see Figure 5). We will discuss this in more depth later in the book.

Perhaps the twin stars of Gemini remind us that our current dualistic thinking is only a phase in human consciousness and that, with the return of the Sun to the galactic center, we will remember our underlying unity and common source. Gemini and Sagittarius, in their alignment with the Milky Way, also remind us that our wisdom and knowledge need to be in alignment with the Tree of Life, with the mystery and energies of the universe. When we detach ourselves and view the life around us as objects, rather than as parts of the unified web of life, we end up in distorted ways of thinking and being. Indeed, we then truly find ourselves expelled from the Garden and lost in our own sense of alienation and separation. When we look to the image of the twins, individual in their identity but intrinsically interconnected, standing facing the life-giving path of the Milky Way, we find our way back to the Garden and to deep connection with all of life.

CHAPTER SEVEN

THE AGE OF TAURUS (4420-2260 BCE)

Taurus, the Bull, began to rise at the time of the spring equinox in about 4420 BCE and heralded a period in which the Bull was honored as sacred. In Egypt, the cult of Hathor (the celestial cow goddess) was prominent (Grasse, *Signs of the Times*, p. 10). The Phoenicians worshiped "El," the bull-god (Brady, *Brady's Book of Fixed Stars*, p. 229). The cult of the Bull spread throughout the ancient cultures, including Sumer, India, and Crete.

In classical astrology, Taurus is known as an earth sign. During this time in prehistory, the use of agriculture spread, and oxen were domesticated. This age marked the end of the Neolithic period and movement into the Bronze Age (around 3500-3000 BCE), when metalworking became more prevalent.

The Age of Taurus at its outset was a period when the Earth was viewed as sacred, and goddess cultures flourished in ancient Europe and throughout the Middle East. The sign Taurus is ruled by Venus, and many ancient cultures honored this planet as a primary deity. For example, in ancient Sumer during the Age of Taurus, the principal deity was Inanna, later known in Babylonian times as Ishtar. Both relate to Venus and her cycle of movement in the sky from evening star to morning star.

Archetypally, in traditional astrology, Venus relates to what we value. It is about our deep relationship with nature and with sexuality and procreation. Venus in ancient times was portrayed as a goddess of fertility and love. Interestingly, in some cultures, for example, among the Mayans, Venus was also viewed as a goddess of war. The ancient Mayans timed their battles with the heliacal rising of Venus (i.e., when Venus was first seen rising before the Sun). We will explore later how this association of Venus with war may relate to the Venus cycle and to the different cultural understandings of Venus as a morning and evening star.

This latter facet of Venus and the Age of Taurus may be related, in part, to the nature of the sub-age, Scorpio (3340-2260 BCE), which carries the energy of its traditional ruler, Mars. Interestingly, this sub-age correlates with the movement from the Neolithic Age into the Bronze Age, when metalworking, including the formation of weapons, became more prominent. The sign Scorpio relates to the themes of death, passion, and deep transformation. While Taurus relates to what is tangible and seen, Scorpio relates to what is unseen, beneath the surface, culturally taboo. The polarity of Taurus and Scorpio also relates to the use or misuse of power.

The themes of the Age of Taurus, related to this polarity, demonstrate a struggle that began to take place as to how we would be in relation to nature. Was the Earth to be honored as sacred and treated with respect or was the Earth meant to be controlled, tamed, and subdued? In this age, we also see a shift in the relationship between men and women from one of equality to the power imbalance of patriarchy. War began to spread as the themes of power and dominance came to the fore.

As with all of the archetypal polarities that the signs and planets represent, they do not indicate predestination or fate but rather relate to the themes of the times. As humans, we are able to exert our free will and choose to live out the deeper meaning or manifest the shadow side of these archetypes.

At the outset of this period, the peaceful goddess cultures flourished. These cultures valued equality, cooperative relationships, and creativity (as is evident in the beauty of the art and monuments of this time). As the age unfolded, it also was a time of dramatic change. During this period, the Kurgan nomadic tribes began to invade the cultures of the Mediterranean and ancient Europe, bringing a radically different lifestyle. From about 4400 to 3000 BCE, they brought about a shift from agriculture to nomadic herding and from a more egalitarian, peaceful form of society to the beginning of patriarchal culture.

What happened that led to this profound cultural shift? How is it that the Old European cultures honoring the Earth goddess were overtaken by patriarchal "sky-god" cultures? One fascinating hypothesis put forward by two British astronomers, Victor Clube and William Napier, as well as by Mike Baillie, an Irish paleoecologist, is that our planet has experienced profound catastrophic encounters with debris from comet activity (or "cosmic swarms") related, ironically enough, to the Taurid complex, the comet debris that the Earth passes through in late fall and early summer. The research conducted by these scientists as well as others indicates that there have been several periods of catastrophic environmental and climatic change have occurred across the past five thousand years. These dates include; 2911 BCE, 2345 BCE, 1628 BCE, 1159 BCE, 208 BCE, and AD 536.

Evidence from tree rings, ice-core samples, and historical and mythological records all point to the probability of widespread destruction resulting from comet activity. When cometary debris explodes in our atmosphere or on the surface of the Earth, it results in massive destruction including volcanic activity, earthquakes, flooding, poisonous ocean outgassing, dust clouds, and widespread famine and death. Moe Mandelkehr, who has compiled the archeological, climatological, and geological evidence for the period around 2300 BCE, has written:

> The archeological evidence sets forth two significant phenomena that took place at or about 2300 B.C. First, a large number of sites were destroyed by earthquake and conflagration, over a large land area encompassing all of the known advanced cultures at that time. Second, cultural changes occurred, not only in the areas of destroyed sites, but over the entire Earth.
>
> (Baillie, *Exodus to Arthur: Catastrophic Encounters with Comets*, p. 148)

Benny Peiser, in the article "Comets and Disaster in the Bronze Age" in the *Journal of the Council of British Archeology* (December 1997, pp. 6-7), writes:

> At some time around 2300 B.C., give or take a century or two, a large number of major civilizations of the world

collapse, simultaneously it seems. The Akkadian in Mesopotamia, the Old Kingdom of Egypt, the Early Bronze civilization in Israel, Anatolia and Greece, as well as the Indus Valley civilization in India, the Hilmand civilization in Afghanistan and the Hongshan culture in China, the first urban civilizations in the world, all fell into ruin at more or less the same time.

(Peiser, p. 6)

Peiser goes on to note a similar collapse in world cultures around 1200 BCE (for example, the Mycenaeans of Greece, the Hittites of Anatolia, the Egyptian New Kingdom, Late Bronze Age Israel, and the Shang Dynasty of China) (see Peiser, p. 6). It has only been in the last fifteen years that researchers have begun to realize that the widespread destruction was not due to military or human activity but due to dramatic climactic and environmental changes (e.g., earthquakes, eruptions, tidal waves, fires and famines) (see Peiser, p. 7) related to comet activity. The catastrophic effects of the comet activity led to periods of cultural destruction and dissolution, including the Dark Ages, and they coincide with the Hindu yuga cycle, speaking of that time as a low point in human consciousness.

In addition, Baillie posits that the exodus of the Hebrews from Egypt occurred in 1628 BCE and coincided with a period of comet activity and the concomitant eruption of the Santorini volcano. He equates the imagery depicting this event in 1 Chronicles (including the pestilence and death in Israel and Egypt, the parting of the sea, the "Angel of the Lord" in the sky, and the "pillar of cloud" guiding the Israelites) with the sight of the comet and subsequent earthquakes, death, and volcanic eruption in the region. He also notes that the name of the Israelites' God "Yahweh," traditionally interpreted as "I am that I am," can also mean "the storm god," the destroyer, or "he who causes to fall rain and thunder from the heavens" (see Baillie, *Exodus to Arthur: Catastrophic Encounters with Comets*, pp. 115-116).

Baillie, as well as Clube and Napier (see *The Cosmic Serpent*), also attributes the worldwide environmental and cultural crises of AD 540 and the Black Death in Europe in AD 1347 to comet activity. Related to the period of crisis in AD 540 in Europe is the sudden shift in religious orientation from pagan beliefs and practices in Ireland to Christianity shortly after this period. Saint Patrick, either a real or mythological figure, is thought to have lived in this time and was the one to drive out the "serpents" from Ireland. In that there are no snakes in Ireland, could the reference to "serpents" be an allusion to comets, often depicted across cultures as "serpents" or "dragons"? It is also significant to note that Brigid, the fire goddess of Ireland, whose death is dated at AD 525, is known as the "fiery dart" or "arrow of fire." Perhaps these references associate her with this appearance of fiery comet activity in the sky at about this same time (see Baillie, *Exodus to Arthur: Catastrophic Encounters with Comets*, pp. 131-135).

The increasing evidence from astronomy, archeology, dendrochronology, and geology points to these significant periods of environmental and cultural crisis. These climatic and global crises correlate with the periods in prehistory (2911 BCE and 2345 BCE) when the dramatic shift from the goddess cultures to "sky god" cultures took place. The "sky god" cultures were characterized by a shift from honoring of the Earth to a fear of a transcendent and punishing God in the sky. This God required sacrifice, penance, and obedience in order to avoid his wrath and judgment. Could it be that the fear evoked by these terrifying cometary impacts led to this cultural shift from matrilineal, earth-honoring goddess cultures to the patriarchal, "sky god" cultures?

Another major celestial event was also occurring during this age. Beginning in about 2700 BCE, the celestial north polestar began to shift from Alpha Draconis in the Draco constellation to Polaris (which is our current celestial polar star in the Northern Hemisphere). As we shall see later, this change was reflected in some of the myths of the time noting the uprooting of the cosmic tree holding Earth and sky together. This period in prehistory was a time of dramatic change, emanating from the sky and activating profound earth changes.

Returning to the archetypal themes of this age, classically, the sign Taurus is associated with the throat and with creativity. So it is significant that the first writing (cuneiform) appeared during this period in Sumer (around 2700 BCE) and then shortly after in the hieroglyphic writing of ancient Egypt. It is also the period in which the Egyptian Book of the Dead was compiled to address the journey through death to rebirth (Scorpio). It was also when the I Ching emerged in preliterate form in China, addressing issues of life, duality, and the origin of the world

(Taurus). Due to the development of writing in this period, we have the benefit of written mythology to examine the themes of this age and later ones in more depth.

One of the first known written myths from the historical period is from ancient Sumer and is the story of the goddess Inanna. Inanna was queen of heaven, daughter of the moon god and was identified with the planet Venus. This myth chronicles the Venus cycle in which Venus appears as an evening star for approximately 260 days, and then disappears beneath the horizon for about 3 to 7 days, and then reemerges as a morning star for approximately 260 days. Venus returns to its point of origin after eight years (and five synodic cycles), making the numbers 5 and 8 sacred to Venus. The image of the pentacle is associated with Venus, and in ancient times, Venus was often depicted as an eight-petaled flower.

The myth of Inanna follows the Venus cycle and explores the meaning and mystery of this pattern of evolution from evening star, descent and subsequent return as morning star. The themes of life, death, and rebirth reflect the meaning of the Taurus/Scorpio polarity. In addition, the myth also describes the changes that were occurring in the sky and in the culture during that time. The oldest tablets of the myth date from 2000 BCE, but the story was thought to be a part of an oral tradition most likely dating back to about 3000 BCE. Within the Inanna cycle is the Sumerian creation story. In this tale, we see evidence of the increasing dualities within the culture between men and women, the upper world and the lower world and the Earth and sky. Formerly, in the Sumerian language, the world was described as "heaven-earth" (Kramer, *Sumerian Mythology*, p. 41), or the unified sphere of the dome of the sky and the Earth below. The myth of Inanna demonstrates the increasing separation between the two, as well as a split in the formerly unified goddess, as can be seen in the passage below:

> In the first days when everything needed was brought into
> being...
> And earth had separated from heaven...
> When the Sky God, An, had carried off the heavens...
> When the Queen of the Great Below, Ereshkigal, was given
> The underworld for her domain...
> (Wolkstein and Kramer, *Inanna:*
> *Queen of Heaven and Earth*, p. 4)

The story also depicts the uprooting of the World Tree, the cosmic tree holding Earth and sky together.

> The whirling South Wind arose, pulling at its roots
> And ripping at its branches
> Until the waters of the Euphrates carried it away.
> (Wolkstein and Kramer, p. 5)

The still point in the heavens was shifting during this age as the celestial polestar was moving from Thuban to Polaris. The storm in the myth may also refer to the upheavals in 2911 BC and 2345 BC with the cataclysmic effects of comet activity.

The story continues with Inanna taking the uprooted tree and planting it in her garden. "She settled the earth around the tree with her foot" (Wolkstein and Kramer, p. 5). Inanna, the queen of heaven, was reestablishing stability in the world by replanting the cosmic tree. However, as the tree grew, Inanna was troubled about some creatures residing in the tree. There is "a serpent who could not be charmed," an Anzu bird, and the "dark maid Lilith," who built her home in the trunk (Wolkstein and Kramer, p. 6). As the story unfolds, Inanna calls on the aid of the warrior Gilgamesh, who banishes the unwanted inhabitants and forms a throne and bed for Inanna from the tree.

If we remember that these images (the serpent, bird, and Lilith) were strongly associated with the ancient Neolithic bird and serpent goddess traditions, we begin to see the significance of the events in the story. The myth described both the radical shift in the sky and what was occurring culturally. "As above, so below." The winged serpent (the constellation Draco), which had represented one of the most ancient images of the goddess, was being uprooted from its stable point in the sky as the ways of the sacred feminine began to be devalued culturally. The unified goddess holding the mystery of life and death, of order and chaos, was being split into the goddess of the great above and the goddess of the great below in the same way that the Earth and sky were increasingly seen as separate entities. Perhaps, as was stated before, this split began with the transition from the Age of Gemini into the Age of Taurus and the separation of the ecliptic from the Milky Way. The split also echoes the themes of the Taurus/Scorpio polarity of what is seen and what is unseen (i.e., the realm of the invisible, of the repressed, and of death).

As we move further into the Inanna story, we see some of the themes of the Age of Taurus, including an honoring of nature and of sensuality. Inanna speaks with her brother, the Sun god, Utu, about her longing to wed. The story demonstrates the passion and pleasure associated with sexuality that is a characteristic of the archetypal meaning of Taurus (associated with the energies of the Earth and embodied spirituality) as Inanna celebrated the desires of her body.

> My vulva, the horn,
> The Boat of Heaven,
> Is full of eagerness like the young Moon.
> My untilled land lies fallow.
> (Wolkstein and Kramer, p. 37)

Later in the story, Inanna and Utu argue about who would be her lover. Inanna wanted a farmer: "The man of my heart works the hoe. The farmer! He is the man of my heart!" (Wolkstein and Kramer, p. 32). However, Utu convinced her to choose Dumuzi, the shepherd: "Sister, marry the shepherd. Why are you unwilling? His cream is good; his milk is good. Inanna, marry Dumuzi" (Wolkstein and Kramer, pp. 32-33). We see in this struggle the shifting in the Middle East from the primacy of agriculture to the dominance of the nomadic shepherds who were invading the land.

In the central part of the myth, Inanna hears the call from the "great below" and sets out on a journey to the underworld to visit her sister, Ereshkigal, who had been banished to the world below. In other myths, the banishment of Ereshkigal was attributed to her having been raped and abused. Ereshkigal originally represented the ancient grain goddess, the unified goddess of life and death and harvest. Now, she has become the underworld goddess split off from her sister, the queen of heaven. In the story, Inanna traveled to visit her sister because Gugalanna ("the bull of heaven") was dying. This story signifies the awareness of the Sumerians that the constellation Taurus, the Bull, was sinking below the horizon in the east at the time of the vernal equinox.

As the myth continues, Inanna is challenged at the gate to the underworld and has to go through seven gates as part of her descent. Following the pattern of Venus in the sky, she journeys through seven gates to the underworld as the planet Venus goes through seven conjunctions with the crescent balsamic Moon in her evening star phase. When Inanna finally encounters her sister, Ereshkigal, in the depths of the underworld (when Venus disappears from view in the sky and is conjunct the Sun), Ereshkigal in her rage and jealousy "fastened on Inanna the eye of death. She spoke against her the word of wrath. She uttered against her the cry of guilt. She struck her. Inanna was turned into a corpse" (Wolkstein and Kramer, p. 60). In this interaction, Inanna faced the violence, rage, and death now attributed to the underworld.

This myth demonstrates that the formerly unified goddess now in this age had been split into Inanna, the queen of heaven and of fertility (Taurus), living in the upper world, and the goddess of death and destruction, Ereshkigal (Scorpio), living in the lower world. In addition, issues of power, violence, and dominance (Scorpio) became important cultural themes in the sub-age as the Kurgan invasions destroyed the goddess cultures and heralded the beginning of patriarchal culture.

In the Sumerian story, Inanna is rescued and resurrected by two androgynous earth creatures sent by Enki, the god of wisdom, from the upper world. After being dead for three days, she is revived and returns to the upper world transformed (Scorpio). Again, she ascends through the seven gates (as in the Venus cycle, the planet re-emerges as a morning star and goes through seven conjunctions with the new Moon). Back in her kingdom, Inanna encounters her consort, Dumuzi (Mars), who has usurped her throne in her absence. Dumuzi ends up being sent to the lower world for six months of the year as his punishment. He too has to undergo the death/rebirth transformation in the great below.

Some of the themes of this Sumerian myth are echoed in the Hebrew creation story (written between the fifth and tenth centuries BCE) in the book of Genesis, in which Adam and Eve are expelled from the Garden of Eden. In partaking of the Tree of the Knowledge of Good and Evil, Adam and Eve became self-conscious and experienced a rupture in their relationship with the Divine. In this story, a serpent was the catalyst for their downfall and was cursed along with them. Again, we see the serpent, an ancient image of female power and regeneration, being transformed into an image of evil, something to be feared and banished.

As the Earth and sky began to be perceived as more separate entities, so also enmity began to infect the relationships between men and women and between humans and the natural world. For the first time, the notion of nature as something to be tamed or controlled began to enter human consciousness. With the sign Scorpio (the sub-age of the Age of Taurus), the archetypal themes are those of power, its use and misuse, and issues of life and death. Significantly, this period also marked the transition into the Kali Yuga (the age in the Hindu tradition linked with degradation in society and spirituality). In addition, 3113 BCE is the starting point of the Mayan long-count calendar fifty-two-hundred-year cycle that ends in AD 2012 and was based on their intricate astronomical knowledge of the Venus cycle.

Another myth coming out of Sumer at the end of this age, which exemplifies these themes, is the epic of Gilgamesh. Gilgamesh was a Sumerian king who lived sometime between 2800 and 2500 BCE. In the tale, he was a hero and a shepherd who was driven and overbearing with the men who worked under him. So the people called on the goddess Aruru, who fashioned a companion for Gilgamesh, someone who could match his strength and energy. She created the warrior Enkidu, a natural man who lived in the wild and related more easily to animals than to humans. Again, we see the increasing split between culture and nature. Where once humans and the natural world were part of a unified whole, now there was an increasing sense of duality and division. In the story, Enkidu is lured into a friendship with Gilgamesh (and into society) by being seduced by the harlot Shamhat. As he became more enculturated, he lost his intimate connection with the animals. After being with the harlot:

> [Enkidu] set his face towards the open country of his cattle.
> The gazelles saw Enkidu and scattered,
> The cattle of open country kept away from his body.
> Enkidu had been diminished; he could not run as before.
> Yet he had acquired judgment, had become wiser.
> (Dalley, *Myths of Mesopotamia*, p. 56)

Echoing the themes of the creation story in Genesis, Enkidu became more self-conscious and entered into a new way of being in relation to nature, which was more separate and estranged.

Later in the story, Gilgamesh and Enkidu went on an adventure to destroy the monster, Huwawa, who guarded the great forest. Again, the theme of the intensifying struggle between humanity and nature is portrayed. After destroying Huwawa, Gilgamesh was asked by Ishtar (the later Babylonian version of the Sumerian goddess Inanna) to marry her. After Gilgamesh rejected her, Ishtar set the bull of heaven on the two companions. Enkidu slayed the bull. Again, we have the reference to the death of the Bull, the shifting of the Taurus constellation from the vernal equinox. Enkidu then was sentenced to death by the gods.

Gilgamesh, overwhelmed with grief and his own fear of death, set off to find Utnapishtim, who dwelled at the entrance to the eternal realm and could tell him how to find the herb of immortality. In his quest, Gilgamesh arrived at the pass of the mountain of Mashu ("Twins"), "whose peaks reach as high as the banks of heaven, whose breast reaches down to the underworld; the scorpion people keep watch at its gate, those whose radiance is terrifying and whose look is death, whose frightful splendor overwhelms mountains, who at the rising and setting of the Sun keep watch over the Sun" (de Santillana and von Dechend, *Hamlet's Mill,* p. 293; translation by Heidel).

De Santillana and von Dechend speculate that this description is a reference to the constellation Scorpius (associated with the sign Scorpio) and the twin stars Lambda Ypsilon. Yet, it might be equally valid to interpret this description as describing the arc of the Milky Way from its end in Gemini (the "Twins") to the other end at Sagittarius and near Scorpius. As was stated earlier, the galactic center is located near the constellations of Sagittarius and Scorpius and is "guarded" by the scorpion people. The image of the scorpion (Scorpius) as the guardian of the gate to immortality is evident in many ancient cultures, including ancient Egypt (seen as Selket) and among the ancient Mayans (see de Santillana and von Dechend, *Hamlet's Mill,* p. 295).

While Gilgamesh eventually was aided in finding the immortal realm and diving deep into the dark waters to retrieve the herb of immortality, he lost it at the end of the story when it was snatched away by a serpent (literally translated as "earth-lion" (see de Santillana and von Dechend, p. 300). Perhaps part of the moral of this tale was to remind the people that, though society might increasingly strive to explore and know the realms of nature and the cosmos, our efforts to be in control of life and death and the laws of the universe would ultimately end in futility.

At the same time, this tale clearly refers to the critical solstice and equinox points during the Age of Taurus, with the vernal equinox in Taurus, the autumnal equinox in Scorpius, the winter solstice point in Aquarius, and the summer solstice in Leo. These points formed the critical "poles" of this age (featuring the fixed signs) and will be important as we look at our current movement into the Age of Aquarius.

As we reflect on this age, we are struck by the intensity of the Earth changes and cultural shifts of this period and the increasing polarization and separation of Earth and sky, male and female, light and dark, and life and death, and of the notions of good and evil. Yet, when we remember that every age is a part of the larger cycle of the Great Year, we honor the mystery of the learning that was unfolding in our human consciousness in this time of turmoil and dualities.

As the Age of Taurus ends with the destruction of the goddess cultures and the shift into the patriarchal and historical period, we enter the Age of Aries.

CHAPTER EIGHT

THE AGE OF ARIES (2260-100 BCE)

Aries is the constellation of the Ram and in traditional astrology is ruled by the planet Mars. Both the sub-age of Scorpio (ending the age of Taurus) and the beginning of the Age of Aries are ruled by Mars. This is a period in human history in which warfare became a dominant aspect of culture. With the rise in patriarchy came the increase in warrior cultures. The sub-age of Aries is Libra (1180 – 100 BCE), which is ruled by Venus. Across the two ages (of Taurus and Aries), we see the interplay of Mars and Venus evidenced in the shifting nature of gender relationships and the tension between the valuing of connection (cooperative relationship) versus that of dominance (power over). This tension and dynamic was seen throughout cultures in social policy and practice, in interpersonal relationships, and in the societal views of nature.

This theme is also a part of the polarity of the archetypal meanings of the signs of Aries and Libra. In traditional astrology, Aries is a cardinal fire sign. It is the energy of assertion, the longing for independence, for experiencing the self as a separate entity. Libra, in contrast, is about balance, harmony, and mutuality in relationship. We see throughout the Age of Aries this tension between the increasing assertion of individuality and the effort to maintain a sense of harmonious relationships in the society through the imposition of law and forms of justice. The themes of the Libra sub-age relate to how we engage in society with each other, how we define justice and find a way of coexisting in order and harmony.

In the Age of Aries, the cult of the bull of the former age was gradually replaced with that of the ram. The sacrifice of lambs and rams as ceremonial practice was prevalent throughout many cultures. In Egypt, there was a shift from the bull-god, Montu, to the ram-god, Amon. As is typical with the shifting of ages, the imagery and cultic practices of the past age were denigrated. In the Age of Aries, images of bull slayings became prominent; for example, in the Mithraic religion of Persia. In the Hebrew account of Moses descending from Mount Sinai with the Ten Commandments, he sternly criticized the people for their worship of the golden calf (Grasse, *Signs of the Times,* p. 11).

In contrast to the more Earth-centered spirituality of the Age of Taurus, in the Age of Aries (a fire sign), fire ceremonies became a critical part of religious practice. For example, in the Hebrew Bible, Moses met Yahweh in the fire. Also during this age, Zoroastrianism focused on the importance of fire rituals.

In this age, with Aries and its traditional astrological association with the head (and mental activity) as well as with leadership, we see the increase in the codification of culture with laws; for example, those established in the Hebrew Torah and the code of Hammurabi in Babylon (2081 BCE). The Vedic texts were also developed in this period by the Aryans invading India. These texts emphasize hierarchy and the class structure of the society. These codified laws show a shift from an understanding of natural law to the imposition of human law.

In India, Indra, the war-god was a prominent deity. Toward the end of this Age, the Hindu Upanishads emerged (650 BCE) as well as the Chinese Taoist philosopher, Lao-Tzu (531 BCE), and Buddha was born in 528 BCE. These seeded many of the spiritual ideas that flourished in the next age, Pisces.

Many empires arose during this age in Egypt, Greece, China, and Rome. Alexander the Great in Greece was depicted with ram's horns on his head (Grasse, p. 11). The rise of the Roman Empire came at the end of this age (around 510 BCE). These empires reflected the Aries archetype of the warrior and the need for conquest and control.

It is also in this age that we see the shift from right-brain dominance to more left-brain ways of thinking and knowing. With the increasing development of the cerebral cortex, the self-conscious and separatist ways of thought and of being increased. Prior to this, with more right-brain dominance, humans experienced themselves as part of the larger whole of life around them, relating to other life forms in an intuitive, empathic, and even telepathic manner. As the shift into the Age of Aries brought an increase in self-assertion and individualism, the left-brain way of defining reality in a more detail-oriented and linear manner became more prominent. Individual consciousness increased, as did the efforts to structure the laws and social mores of society. These developments also led to an increase in power struggles and efforts by leaders to dominate, rather than the former more egalitarian modes of governance characterizing the earlier pre-patriarchal communities.

In part, this shift from right-brain dominance to left-brain dominance may have been due to the development and use of written language. As Leonard Shlain has written in *The Alphabet and the Goddess*, written language led to the increasing dominance of the left hemisphere, which controls the speech and language sections of the brain. Interestingly, the most ancient written languages were pictorial, such as the cuneiform texts and hieroglyphics. Also, these languages were written from the right to left, as you might expect in people who were more right-brain dominant (and most likely had a left-handed dominance as a result). However, over time, language became more symbolic and abstract and shifted to being written from left to right as people became more left-brain dominant (with an increased propensity for right-handedness).

It is also interesting to note that the ancient prehistoric cultures were more lunar in their orientation and intimately connected with the movement of the Moon in the sky (which grows in size from right to left). In contrast, in our solar cultures, we are very attuned to the movement of the Sun, rising in the east (in the left from our human perspective) and setting in the west (right), so the directional orientation of the languages may reflect these cultural attunements.

Along with this shift to more left-hemispheric dominance came the increase in linear, analytical, and abstract ways of thinking. These changes resulted in an increasing development of human law (as opposed to natural law) and an increasing disconnection from nature. In this era, people began to separate themselves from a sense of unity with the natural world and to analyze the world around them in the context of objective thinking or the perspective of self and object. It is also during this period that dualistic thinking became more prevalent.

Interestingly enough, this is also the age when even our orientation to the movement of the stars in the sky reflected this increasing separation from nature. The modern Western tropical zodiac was fixed in time in the Age of Aries when the sun was rising in Aries at the spring equinox. In this way, the constellations and signs of the zodiac began to take on separate meanings as the signs became more reflective of the seasonal changes and time of year rather than the actual positions of the stars in the sky. The sidereal zodiac, which more accurately reflects the placement of the constellations, is now twenty-three degrees different from the tropical zodiac due to the precessional shifting of the zodiac one degree every seventy-two years. While the precessional process continued, the mental constructs of the signs of the zodiac in Western thought became fixed in place and no longer coincided with the constellations bearing those names.

In the Age of Aries (in which the Sun is exalted), we also see the shift from lunar cultures to solar cultures. There was a transition from a reverence for the Earth to deification of the sky and the sky gods. With right-brain dominance, the experience of the Divine was immanent; it was present in all of creation, in all of life. With the shift to left-brain dominance, spirit became separated from nature and the Divine was viewed as transcendent, above us, apart from us. In this way, the experience of the Divine was sought through propitiation, through sacrifice, and through guidance from external authorities, and it was no longer seen as an intrinsic part of the human and natural experience. This time was also characterized by the transition from the honoring of the great goddess to the image of a male god as the dominant deity. The goddess cultures continued to be destroyed during this period and were replaced by nomadic, herding patriarchal cultures.

A story that is at the heart of the Jewish and Islamic (and later Christian) traditions arising in this age is that of Abraham, known as the father of the Israelites through his son Isaac, and as the father of the Arabs through his son Ishmael. Originally, known as Abram, "high/exalted father/leader" (in Hebrew), he later was named Abraham, meaning "father/leader of many." In the Qur'an (Koran), he is portrayed as a founding prophet. In both the Hebrew Bible and in the

Qur'an, Abraham was called to sacrifice his son in obedience to God and was later blessed as the father of his people and future generations. In the Hebrew Bible, this sacrifice foreshadowed the Christian story of the sacrifice of Jesus, God's son, for the life and salvation of the people. While the historicity of Abraham has not been definitively proven, research places his birth circa 1812 BCE within the Jewish traditions or around 2166 BCE by other calculations, either at or near the beginning of this age.

In the Hebrew version of this story (from Genesis 22 of the Old Testament), God tested Abraham by asking him to sacrifice his son. God told Abraham to take his only son Isaac to a mountaintop and offer him up as a burnt offering. Abraham complied and took wood, fire, a knife, and his son to the mountain as God instructed. There, Abraham built an altar. He bound Isaac and laid him on the wood on the altar and reached for his knife to slay him. Before Abraham killed his son, the angel of God stopped him, saying:

> "Abraham… Do not lay your hand on the lad… for now I
> know that you fear God, seeing you have not withheld your
> son, your only son, from me… because you have done this…
> I will indeed bless you, and I will multiply your descendants
> as the stars of the heavens and as the sand which is on the
> seashore… because you have obeyed my voice."
>
> (Genesis 22: 12, 15-18, Revised
> Standard Version)

Of significance in this story are the themes of obedience to a transcendent Father God and the importance of sacrifice. Prior to this age, there was a stronger sense of the interconnection of Earth and sky and of deity as immanent, manifesting in nature and in an embodied manner. The holy places were caves and places such as wells or rivers that held the energy of the sacred Earth. In this age, there was a shift toward the notion of a sky god who was worshipped on the mountaintops and high places. This story also marks the transition into patriarchy, where the lineage was no longer through the women (matrilineal) but was now through the father line (patrilineal). In addition, there is the theme of separation and individuation as Abraham was called away from his community to face his individual test from God, and he was asked to be willing to sever the commitment to his human son to obey the transcendent Father God. In the story, God released Abraham from having to slay his son and offered a ram to be sacrificed in his stead (Genesis 22:13), again reflecting the cult of the ram of this age.

With the Israelites, the notion of monotheism emerged. From a lineage of polytheism and the worship of many deities came the idea of the one God, Yahweh, to be worshipped over all others. A few thousand years later, it is difficult for us to conceive how radical this belief was at that time and how it led to a separation of the Israelites from the surrounding peoples who, according to the Judaic tradition, worshipped "false gods." Again, the theme of separation became prominent in this age.

As separation and individuation came into the collective consciousness, so also did the idea of "sin" or "evil." In the Hebrew Bible, sin originated out of the human consciousness of separation from God as Adam and Eve ate of the Tree of Knowledge of Good and Evil (Genesis 3). In eating the fruit of the tree, Adam and Eve became self-conscious and experienced themselves as separate from God (Genesis 3:7-8). Evil then inherently refers to the sense of separation, of division, and of duality. Sacrifice became the ritual practice to provide propitiation for that rupture and to allow renewed union between humanity and divinity. The polarity of Aries (the notion of individuality and oneness) and Libra (relationship) are again dominant in these cultural and religious themes. What is significant is that the unity and communion with nature and spirit which were once a given in human experience became increasingly elusive and were sought after through obedience, sacrifice and devotion to a transcendent God.

This change also was reflected in the shift from a lunar culture to a solar culture. Heinrich Zimmer explained the impact of this shift in India:

> The recurrent phases of the Moon were a visible pledge of eternally renewed rebirth. But this lunar era of the human spirit with its hope of immortality grounded in perpetual alternation, gave way to the solar era, when the unchanging eternity of solar existence was promised to those initiated through "knowledge." The Moon, formerly a symbol of the supreme consolation and visible hope, now came to stand for the nightmarish vicious circle of death and birth,

when only an esoteric "knower" could escape into a higher transcendent world.

(Zimmer, Man and Transformation, <u>Eranos</u>, p. 348)

The Moon was exalted in the Age of Taurus while in the Age of Aries, the Sun became exalted.

The sub-age of Aries is Libra. In this way, the sign of Libra, ruled by Venus, offered a possible balance to the individualism and assertion of the ego fostered by Aries. Libra, an air sign associated with the longing for balance, harmony, and mutuality in relationship, is able to bring to the Aries' emphasis on the self an awareness of the needs and concerns of others. Each age contains its balancing archetypal polarity in the meaning of the opposite sign; however, if the deeper meaning and energy of a sign are not integrated at the beginning of the age, then the distortions are likely to continue into the sub-age. This seems to be the case with the historical period of the Libra sub-age of Aries. At the end of this age, we see the movement toward the Dark Ages and the nadir of human culture and development with an overemphasis on materialism, individualism, violence and wars for power, land, and wealth. The out-of-balance Aries energy from the beginning of the age became channeled into interaction with others (Libra) in a destructive manner and in a quest for dominance.

If we reflect on the deeper archetypal themes and learning of this age, it is perhaps a reminder to us to integrate the assertion of self with a concern for the needs and welfare of others and to bring the exploration of the individuated self and ego into balance, attunement and respect for our interdependence with the natural world and with others. In integrating the energies of Mars and Venus, we come to understand the balance of the sacred masculine and sacred feminine and of our individuality with our sense of community and communion with all of life. In this integration, we also are able to move beyond the polarities of spirit as immanent (as is seen in the more ancient Earth-based, goddess spiritualities) and spirit as transcendent (as is evident in most patriarchal religious belief systems) to an understanding that spirit is both in all of life and beyond any form.

CHAPTER NINE

THE AGE OF PISCES (100 BCE – AD 2060)

The Age of Pisces is symbolized by the constellation of the two fish swimming in different directions, the eastern one swims upward while the western fish aligns with the ecliptic. According to Bernadette Brady, Pisces and Aries merge in the sky because "there was never a clear distinction between these two constellations, as Pisces is so large, its two Fish reaching through the sky actually encompass the stars of Aries" (Brady, *Brady's Book of Fixed Stars,* p. 311). The symbol of the fish was ancient. It denoted wisdom and was associated with the image of the yoni (womb, source of life). For example, in ancient China, the goddess Kwan-yin was the great mother and "yoni of yonis" and was seen as a fish goddess (Brady, p. 311). It is not surprising then that classically, this sign has been seen as yin or feminine in its energy.

In astrology, Pisces is a mutable water sign coming at the end of the cycle of the zodiac. Archetypally, its themes pertain to the surrender of the self, of the ego, to some larger vision or purpose. Traditionally ruled by Jupiter, it relates to faith and spiritual beliefs. Many of the religious ceremonies developed in this age involved the ritual use of water, such as for baptisms and for blessings. Later, Neptune became the modern ruler of Pisces and relates to that longing to merge with the cosmic oneness, with the sea of consciousness, with source. Neptune also relates to our longing to redeem ourselves, to recover from the sense of separation, and to restore our relationship with the Divine.

The Piscean Age was characterized by the rise of the great religions of Christianity, Islam, Buddhism, and Confucianism, calling on people to commit themselves to a larger purpose. Buddha was born in 510 BCE setting the stage for this age, and Jesus was born sometime around AD 1 at the time of a major conjunction of Jupiter and Saturn. While the core teachings of both Buddha and Jesus relate to a mystical relationship with spirit, their followers over time institutionalized and codified their teachings, forming the religions of Buddhism and Christianity. Interestingly, the symbol for Christianity across the past two thousand years has been the fish, and Jesus was referred to as a "fisher of men."

Following the sense of separation and individuation arising from the previous age, the message of Jesus and Buddha and of other teachers of this age was one of mystical communion, of merger with the Divine. Throughout this era, there is an emphasis on mysticism and dissolution into a larger sense of service to and identity with spirit. Perhaps this was a corrective to the separatism of the previous age, but it is noteworthy that the theme was primarily of the *Individual* soul attempting to merge with the Divine. The mystical notion of this time is that spirit or love permeates all life and the entire universe and that if the self can dissolve and let go of the boundaries of individuality, there can be a return to that sense of oneness. This is the dissolving that Pisces offers, the death of the ego that can lead to rebirth into a greater unity.

In their origins, all of the great religious traditions arising in the Age of Pisces come from these mystical roots. It is the core message of Christianity, Judaism, Hinduism, Buddhism, Taoism, and the Sufi path of Islam. Jesus taught that "God is love," and in the Vedic tradition, Atman (analogous to the soul) is Brahman (of divinity). All of these traditions emphasize the letting go of the self to merge with divinity and return to a more immanent sense of spirituality. There is also a reemphasis on the mystery and unknowable nature of the Divine. Through our intuition, enlightenment, ecstasy, or the dissolving of our sense of separateness, we can experience (rather than intellectually know or assert) our connection with the Divine.

Of significance is also the theme in this age of the redeemer or savior. This theme fits with the meaning of the traditional planetary ruler of Pisces, which is Jupiter. Archetypally, this planet is associated with characteristics of the teacher, guru, or spiritual leader. At the advent of the Age of Pisces, there was an "extraordinary proliferation of redeemer cults ... which spread with a mystical intensity quite unknown to the ancient world at any previous epoch" (Greene, *The Astrological Neptune and the Quest for Redemption*, p. 71). These cults included those of the early Gnostics and involved competing redeemer/ saviors, including Mithras, Orpheus, and Jesus. These cults viewed the cosmos as a battleground between the powers of darkness and light and between matter and spirit. In their quest for redemption, their practices focused on "a preoccupation with perfectionism, visionary experience, sexual abstinence and martyrdom." Unlike the cults of the bull and the ram in which sacrifice was often done to ensure fertility for the land and the people, sacrifice in this age took on an even greater emphasis as a form of propitiation for separation from the Divine and an abnegation of the body to bring greater union with the pure realm of spirit.

This form of sacrifice is very evident in the story of the crucifixion of Jesus in the Christian tradition. Embedded in this tradition was a sense of the body and the realm of earthly matter as the source of separation and sin. Practices to transcend or release the spirit from the body became the focus, and the duality between the realms of spirit and of flesh was encoded in the religious ideology. This dualism and its concomitant effects characterized the nature of this age. Initially, at the outset of the age, the emphasis was on the effort to reestablish union with the Divine through mystical "knowing" and through sacrifice and transcendence of the realm of body and matter. Later in the age, the realm of spirit began to be denied and devalued with the resulting idealization of the realm of the mind and obsession with the efforts to control the physical world around us.

As the Age of Pisces moved into the sub-age of Virgo, the earlier mystical traditions became more codified and institutionalized as religious systems, such as those of Buddhism, Islam and Christianity. Virgo is classically known as an earth sign and is ruled by the planet Mercury. Its themes relate to discrimination and mental analysis and are evident in the formation of these religious belief systems. Virgo in its relation to Mercury and analytical thought led to an increasing emphasis, toward the end of the age, on science, technology, and our efforts to comprehend and control our environment and the workings of our body and of nature. It involved harvesting natural resources for our own use. As part of the shadow side of this sign, it also led to an increasing myopic vision (focusing on the "trees" and losing sight of the "forest") and on work and day-to-day reality. In reaction to the Piscean emphasis on spirituality and the dissolution of self, Virgo focused on the primacy of the mind and our capacity to manage our bodies and our environment. This focus is evident in the Copernican revolution of five hundred years ago, which led to our current scientific worldview that emphasizes our intellectual capacities and the human ability to analyze and decipher the nature of the universe.

Virgo in its highest sense is associated with the ancient grain goddess and with the sacred feminine, and it retains a deep connection to Piscean spirituality and cosmic consciousness. The Virgo discrimination in this way can enable us to integrate our connection with spirit into daily reality. Virgo is also the sign of the healer who is able to discern the movement of energy in the body and who understands the complex interactions between body, mind, and spirit.

In addition, Virgo is the sign of the vestal virgin. While this tradition became distorted in patriarchal times, in its more ancient meaning, it related to a deep understanding of sexuality as a pathway to the Divine. Tantric sexuality in it origins was an intimate knowledge of the way in which sacred sexuality is about union and communion. In entering into the fullness of the body and moving into kundalini energy, we move from physical union to a communion with the Divine Spirit. Integrating this Virgo wisdom with the Piscean mysticism might have led to a more fully embodied understanding of spirituality, to a deeper sense of the sacred in our day-to-day reality, and to a richer honoring of the sacredness of the Earth and of all of life around us.

Unfortunately, in the last thousand years, we have seen more of the shadow side of the Virgo archetype in modern Western culture. Virgo in its polarity to Pisces can become the reaction to spirit and an overemphasis on physical, material reality. In fear of the loss of the ego boundaries that is a part of the deep Piscean connection with spirit, Virgo can become the determined effort to maintain an illusion of dominance and control. Discrimination and discernment become obsessive-compulsiveness. The capacity for analysis evolves into the deification of the intellect in the "Age of Reason." The longing to know and to understand the integration of spirit in matter becomes a determination to gain factual information in order to control external resources and events. Instead of wisdom, we focus on gathering data. Instead of communion, we see a fanatical desire for control. Instead of merger, we become mired in materialism. Sexuality no longer is a pathway to the sacred but can become a manipulation of others for personal gain.

We live now with the aftermath of the shadow side of the themes of this age. In religious fundamentalism, the mystical notion of the dissolution of the self into merger with the Divine became distorted into the notion of martyrdom, of the sacrifice of self and the idealization of death, as a path to salvation. Drawing on the themes of the previous age, fundamentalists demonstrate an obsession with the one "true" path and the evangelical need to convince others of their rightness. The shadow side of Pisces is victimhood, martyrdom and the fog of illusion. Rather than mystical awareness leading to greater integration and wholeness, the mystical longing can result in fanaticism, delusion, and destruction.

In addition, the addictions which have become prevalent in Western cultures also relate to the shadow side of the Age of Pisces. When we lose the deep mystical connection with spirit, we seek it in other ways, such as through "spirits" (alcohol), drugs, or other substances that give us a sense of altered consciousness. In our longing for that mystical communion, we may seek it through addictions that momentarily give us that experience of loss of self and dissolution into another way of being. Addictions are the shadow side of the archetypal meaning of Neptune, the modern planetary ruler of Pisces. Rather than responding to addictions through an increased effort for control (Virgo), perhaps we need to see in them the deep hunger for spirit, for nonordinary states of reality, and provide guidance to those caught in addictions as to how to come back into that relationship with spirit in a true rather than illusory way.

Archetypally, the deeper integration of the themes of the Age of Pisces is about the integration of mind, body, and spirit in a way in which we understand that we are a part of the wholeness of life and are in service to the Divine, while honoring the uniqueness of our incarnation and the divinity in everyone and everything around us. The balance of Virgo and Pisces is the integration of being here now in physical form while also celebrating the way in which we are ultimately beyond form and are part of the unity and energy of the cosmos.

CHAPTER TEN

THE AGE OF AQUARIUS (AD 2060–4220)

We are currently moving into the Age of Aquarius. While astrologers debate the exact starting point of this new age, it is clear that we are in the transition from the Age of Pisces into the Age of Aquarius. For thousands of years, cultures around the world have seen this constellation as the "Water-Bearer," pouring the urn of living water toward the Earth.

In Greek mythology, Aquarius is associated with Ganymede who was taken by Zeus to become the cupbearer to the gods. The gods lived on nectar and ambrosia, and it was thought that Ganymede poured ambrosia from his cup. This liquid was known in Sanskrit as "amrita," "the drink of immortality." Aquarius was therefore associated not only with the waters of life but also with the drink of immortality (see Guttman and Johnson, *Mythic Astrology*, p. 347).

In earlier times, in ancient Babylon, Aquarius was linked with the Gilgamesh epic and with Utnapishtim, a character in this myth. In the story, Gilgamesh was distraught after the death of his closest friend, Enkidu. In trying to bring him back from the realm of death, Gilgamesh went in search of the herb of immortality. In the process, he passed through various tests, or trials, each associated with one of the other fixed signs. First, he faced a bull (Taurus) sent by the goddess. Then he fought a pride of lions (Leo). Finally, he had to go through the doorway guarded by the scorpion-men (Scorpio). He descended to the underworld to find Utnapishtim who was the keeper of the herb of immortality.

Utnapishtim was once mortal but was granted immortality because he heeded the Divine message that the world would be destroyed by a flood. As in the later biblical story of Noah, Utnapishtim built a boat and survived the destructive flood. The deities then granted him eternal life. Gilgamesh gained the herb of immortality from Utnapishtim but later lost it as he sought to return to the upper world (see Guttman and Johnson, p. 346) Again, we see the theme of Aquarius as related to the herb of immortality, a life-giving substance.

It is also significant that this myth marked the importance of the four fixed signs (Taurus, Leo, Scorpio, and Aquarius). Many ancient pagan rituals and ceremonies marking the inflow of energy from the sky to the Earth were associated with the times when the Sun was in one of these constellations. In ancient Europe, the cross-quarter holidays were associated with the fixed signs and marked the midpoints between the solstices and equinoxes. These were the pagan holidays of Beltaine, Lammas, Samhain, and Imbolc.

In ancient Egypt, Aquarius rose at the time of sunset when the Nile was flooding, and this constellation was associated with the life-giving nature of these waters, which brought fertility to the Earth. To them, Aquarius was linked with the physical and spiritual waters that renew and fertilize all of life (see Guttman and Johnson, p. 345).

In going back to the earliest cultural known images related to Aquarius, we find Gula, the ancient Sumerian goddess of healing. Temples to Gula and myths related to her date back to 2000 BCE, but she arose out of an even earlier goddess, Bau, who dated back to 3000 BCE or earlier. Gula (and Bau) were both goddesses of fertility and life-giving power as well as of healing. Gula was associated with the herbal healers and healers who could free a person from illness. She was known as the "Lady of Birth and the Mother of Dogs" (Walker, *The Woman's Encyclopedia of Myths and Secrets*, p. 358) and was often represented by dog figurines. She was also the goddess who wrote down a person's destiny at the time of his or her birth. So, in times of illness or crisis, people would beseech Gula for her help, asking her to heal them and extend their lives.

As we enter the Age of Aquarius, we face a global crisis of ecological imbalance. Perhaps the deep association with the healing nature of Aquarius and the connection with the healing herbs have led to the increased interest in herbalism in this time.

The symbol of Aquarius, the zigzag lines, is the ancient symbol for water and is seen on pottery dating back to Paleolithic times, and it honors the life-giving waters. Archeologist Marija Gimbutas noted that it is "the earliest symbolic motif recorded" (Gimbutas, *The Language of the Goddess*, p. 19). Neanderthals used it as far back as 40,000 BCE. In Magdalenian times and in the Neolithic period, it was often found engraved or painted in association with images of the uterus or vulva, linking the symbol for water with the life-giving fluids of women and of the goddess. In Old Europe, this symbol was often painted on water containers, often in conjunction with an image of the face of the goddess, further strengthening the association between water and the goddess. It was often drawn or painted under the breasts of goddesses, signifying the life-giving milk and generative nature of the goddess (Gimbutas, p. 22). It is also interesting to note that many scientists and political leaders have predicted that in the years ahead, conflicts between nations will focus on water rights, and we will be increasingly affected by the diminishing resources of potable water.

In its polarity with Leo, while the sign Leo has to do with the creative expression of the individual, Aquarius is more about the creative expression of community. Leo is about defining and expressing the self, while Aquarius is about finding identity and equality in collaboration and in a group or cultural context. Astrologically, Aquarius is ruled by Saturn (as the traditional ruler) and Uranus (as the modern ruler) and is a fixed air sign.

We will explore the meaning of Saturn and its relationship with Uranus as corulers of this sign later in the book. For now, we will reflect on the archetypal meaning of the modern planetary ruler of Aquarius, Uranus. The planet was discovered by William Herschel in 1781 around the time of the French and American Revolutions, when culturally much of our world was in upheaval and in a time of change. Uranus is an unusual planet in that it defies the established scientific understanding of planetary orbits and movements. While most planets spin on an axis perpendicular to the plane of the ecliptic, Uranus's axis is almost parallel with the ecliptic. Uranus's south pole points almost directly at the Sun, and its polar regions receive more energy from the Sun; yet its equatorial region is hotter than the poles. Unlike other planets, whose magnetic fields are located in the center of the planet, for Uranus, the magnetic field is sixty degrees from the axis of rotation. Scientists are baffled by these patterns, which break the known planetary rules.

In this way, Uranus carries the archetypal energy of the rebel who breaks with tradition. Richard Tarnas, in his book *Prometheus, the Awakener,* equates the meaning of Uranus with Prometheus, whose name means "foresight," and who was the mythic rebel Titan who defied the gods to steal fire for humankind. Prometheus sought to equalize the relationship between humans and the gods by bringing enlightenment to humanity. Uranus therefore holds the energy of freedom from cultural or normative constrictions or traditions and an openness to truth, to diversity, and to unique ways of being.

With Uranus as its modern ruler, Aquarius relates to the ways in which we need to transform our social structures so that they are more authentic, humanitarian, and egalitarian. The energy of Uranus is about shattering illusions and structures that are built on false premises. We can expect that in this coming age, our national boundaries and sectarian identifications will break down as we are called into an understanding of what it means to be a global community.

In addition, archetypally, Uranus is associated with energy, electricity, and innovative technology. In this coming time, we will see a continuing escalation and expansion of our technological understanding and the development of computer technology in particular.

Also, in Uranus's association with energy, we can anticipate an increasing understanding of the energetic nature of all of life. New forms of medicine will be developed that utilize this understanding, as well as new forms of travel. In addition, new sources for renewable and sustainable energy will be discovered. In reconnecting with a sense of energy systems, we will also continue to see a resurgence and further development of ancient healing traditions that are based on an understanding of the body as an energy system (such as in Ayurvedic medicine and traditional Chinese medicine and acupuncture, as well as many shamanic healing traditions).

Another aspect of this deepening understanding of energy will be a return to natural law. Since the Age of Aries, we have been living under human law, which includes our efforts to control nature and to see ourselves as superior to and distinct from the natural world. This approach has led to the widespread destruction of our earthly home as well as leading us into a distorted view of ourselves and our relationship with the world around us. Uranus shatters our illusions and our hubris and brings us back to an awareness of the interconnectedness of all of life and of our being part of this living web. In returning to an understanding of natural law, not only will we have to abandon destructive laws and principles that we have used to construct our modern cultures, but religious systems of thought and practice will also be called into question. Uranus is the lightning bolt that strikes at the heart of institutions and structures that are not built on natural truth but rather are based on false premises or illusions and are out of balance.

What does it mean to reconnect with natural law? It means that we will need to be more open to cultural diversity, much like the way in which nature finds its resilience and strength in biodiversity. We will also need to be open to variations in sexual expression. Aquarius is associated with androgyny as well as with sexual and gender diversity, and it is associated with the understanding that, in nature, sexuality is fluid and often not gender specific. This is true in humans as well. We will have to let go of our false notions of what is "right" and open more fully to accept what is, the broad spectrum of ways of being that we find in the world around us.

We will also need to realize that the gender imbalance of patriarchy, viewing maleness as superior, is an illusion based on the cultural shifts arising from the Age of Aries. It is in fact a recent development in human history and not, as many believe, the way things have always been. In letting go of that illusion, we can recover more of a balance in the relationship between men and women, with a deeper understanding of the complementary differences and strengths that we bring to each other. In this way, Aquarius is linked with a renewed sense of balance between the genders and the return of a connection with the sacred feminine. In the last few decades, we have seen a resurgence in women's spirituality movements and an increasing emphasis on the divine feminine in various religions.

Another facet of natural law is an understanding of balance in nature. When one species becomes dominant or overpopulates an area, nature reasserts itself in some way to bring back a sense of balance and harmony. If we do not heed this natural law of balance, we will begin to die off as a species (either through the increasing spread of illnesses, such as AIDS, cancer, and epidemics or by our own violence towards each other), so that the Earth can regain a sense of natural balance. The meaning of the sign of Aquarius reminds us that we must develop more sustainable ways of living on this Earth in respect for and in balance with the other life forms who share our planet.

Aquarius and Uranus also relate to radical transformation, and we are likely to see rapid, sometimes explosive, changes in our culture, technology, politics, and world situation. Uranus is represented by the "Tower" card in the Tarot. Perhaps we can see the effects of Uranus in the shattering of the twin towers in New York on September 11, 2001. At a deeper level, Uranus, in its shattering of traditional forms and beliefs, is asking us to let go of what is false or superficial in our lives. It calls us to remember our essential being, our deeper truth. In response to the tragedy of 9/11/01, many people opened to a deeper level of self-examination and a broader perspective on the global situation. Many Americans saw, beneath the destructive and abhorrent behavior of the fanatical men who martyred themselves and murdered thousands (an extreme expression of the shadow side of the Piscean Age), a Uranian message about our own culpability for the imbalance of resources and treatment of others in the global community. Others reacted with Saturnian outrage and fiercely attempted to defend the structures and patterns of the past, as well as reemphasizing nationalistic boundaries and loyalties rather than seeing this in a more Aquarian perspective and factoring in the welfare of the global community. The themes of Aquarius emphasize multilateral relationships and cooperation among nations. It is a call for equality and tolerance of diversity. What is demanded of us is a respect and honoring of people of all races, creeds, and religions.

However, the shadow side of Aquarius (a fixed air sign) is intellectual detachment and a fear of change. The overemphasis on the intellect and on control of the Virgo sub-age in modern Western culture could continue as we move into this age. It is significant that in Chinese medicine, the spleen and stomach, representing the earth element, are at the center of the human body and bridge the heavenly qi (energy) and earthly qi. This element is the source of nurturance and the digesting of energy for the human body. It is a reminder that if we disconnect from the earth element and from our relationship with the Earth, we lose our center. In the process, we risk becoming ungrounded and emotionally and spiritually disengaged.

From a more hopeful perspective, in moving from the sub-age of Virgo, an earth sign, to Aquarius, we may regain our perspective and detach from the overly materialistic nature of the industrialized nations. The sign of Aquarius reminds us of the importance of nonattachment and that what is most important is the energy, the spirit, which resides in all of life. Uranus cuts through our illusions of security and self-sufficiency and reminds us that we are a global community linked by common concerns. In this age, we have the opportunity to move from our duality consciousness to unity consciousness.

In the Age of Aries, there was a shift to left-brain dominance along with the increasing development of the neocortex. Now, in the Age of Aquarius, we may see an increasing balance of the functioning of the left and right hemispheres. We need to move beyond the eras in which one hemisphere or the other is dominant. In the earliest cultures, from about 40,000 BCE to 1500 BCE, it was the right hemisphere that was dominant. In these cultures, there was a predominance of peaceful, artistic goddess-honoring cultures with an emphasis on holistic, intuitive, experiential ways of knowing. With the shift into left-brain dominance, there was an increasing development of patriarchy and analytical, linear thinking. Now, in the Age of Aquarius, the challenge is to reintegrate the gifts of both hemispheres, to move beyond duality to a new sense of unity. We need to reweave our holistic, intuitive ways of knowing with our intellectualism, to reintegrate wisdom with knowledge.

Interestingly, in our time, neuropsychologists are aware of the increasing prevalence of what are seen as "disorders" of brain-wave functioning and learning disabilities. One current prevalent problem is bipolar disorder, which involves not only extremes of mood (from mania to depression in the most severe form) but also imbalances in the brain-wave patterns and functioning of the two hemispheres. Perhaps this disorder, in part, is related to the shifts happening in our hemispheric functioning that have not been fully integrated.

Other widely seen difficulties are those of attention and concentration known as Attention Deficit Hyperactivity Disorder (ADHD). What is significant is that this "disorder" is known for the dominance of alpha and theta brain-wave activity in contrast to the beta state, which is the state of focused attention, linear thinking and productive activity. The alpha state is the meditative state, and the theta state is associated with highly creative states and with trance states such as those induced by shamanic journeying to connect with the spiritual realms. Perhaps we need to consider whether the children and adults with this disorder are trying to give us a lesson about our own need to come back into balance, to reintegrate these other brain states and ways of being.

Right-brain functioning is more about being, while left-brain functioning is more about doing. The beta-wave state is highly valued in Western, industrialized cultures emphasizing productivity and linear thought. The alpha- and theta-wave states are emphasized in cultures that value art, altered states of consciousness, and ways of seeking wisdom from the realm of spirit. What if we taught our ADHD children how to engage in shamanic journeying, how to work with the alpha and theta states? What messages might they bring us? How might they teach us to come back into balance neurologically and spiritually?

In the Age of Aquarius, we are called into new ways of being, new states of consciousness. As we then move across the next thousand years toward the second phase of the Age of Aquarius, the Leo sub-age, we are challenged to move into new forms of creativity and self-expression that are integrated with this deeper spiritual understanding, humanitarian concern, and sense of global community.

CONCLUSION

For hundreds of years, our thinking has been shaped by Descartes' notion of "I think, therefore I am" (arising out of the individualism of the Ages of Aries and the overemphasis on the intellect of the Virgo sub-age of the Age of Pisces). We have been overly focused on our intellectual and analytical abilities. Enamored with our increasing technological understanding, we have become more and more myopic, breaking reality down into smaller and smaller units in our effort to know and master the secrets of the universe. In our hubris, we divided the atom and created the potential to destroy ourselves and the world around us. In our hunger for information and knowledge, we have lost our sense of meaning and an understanding of our place in the larger whole. Silently, the sky reminds us of who we are, where we are and calls us back into relationship. "As above, so below." Seeking the wisdom of the stars and planets is not about causation or determinism. The stars do not control our destiny. Instead, they reflect the patterns, the currents of energy, in the cosmos. They remind us of the interconnectedness of all of life.

We live in a symbolic universe. The cosmos is sentient and filled with creative intelligence. Part of the wonder of our human nature is our ability to witness and celebrate that creative intelligence. It is not our consciousness (for all of life has consciousness) but our degree of self-consciousness that sets us apart from other creatures. The extent of our self-consciousness allows us to reflect on our own nature and to see and celebrate the other in the context of deep relationship. We seek to know and be known. We search for the Divine, and the Divine is in search of us. What we need to remember is that the cosmos is in communication with us in every moment. We experience this communication in the patterns of the stars, the movements of nature, and in the stirrings of our own hearts. We are called into relationship by the sight of a bird, the cry of a newborn child or the pain in the eyes of a stranger. If we are open, we can see that the recent Earth changes, such as the severe storms, the flooding, and the earthquakes, are a call to us to awaken to our relationship with the Earth. Our responsibility is to see and hear, to listen and respond. We have the choice, moment by moment, to enter into mutual relationship or to separate ourselves. If we close our eyes and our hearts, we sever ourselves from that attunement and from our source.

The message of Aquarius is a call to remember our source, to honor the living waters of our connection with the creative intelligence of the universe and to remember the living waters of our Earth. Uranus, the ruler of Aquarius, is shattering our illusions and our denial. Uranus calls us back into truth and right relationship. Uranus reminds us of the equality of self and other, the value of diversity, and the need for compassion and tolerance.

How then do we heed the message of this time?

What is most important is our openness. The universe is in communication with us; we have but to open our eyes and ears and hearts and listen.

PART THREE

MOVING INTO THE NEW AGE

CHAPTER ELEVEN

LIMINAL PERIODS: TRANSITIONS BETWEEN AGES

We now live in the cusp between the Age of Pisces and the Age of Aquarius. As the ancients knew, these transitional periods are times of turmoil globally, culturally, and in terms of earth changes, but they are also a period of creativity and of the formation of new forms of consciousness. What is critical is how we respond to this time of change and whether we attempt to cling to the patterns of the past or open to new and unfamiliar ways of being. As astrologer Jeffrey Wolf Green has stated, the archetypal meaning of Uranus, the ruler of Aquarius, is "freedom from the known" (see Green, *Uranus: Freedom from the Known*). We now live in a time of uncertainty, when we sense that the ways in which we have been in control and have formed our sense of identity and security, individually and collectively, are dissolving and shattering. Before any new form can emerge, the old way of being needs to die. This is the story of the caterpillar, the phoenix, of resurrection, and of how new stars and galaxies are born. It is the archetypal pattern of death and rebirth. How do we support ourselves in this time of transformation?

It is important that we hold our understanding of this time in the larger framework of the ages, historically and astrologically. To do so allows us to understand the deeper meaning and purpose of this time of turmoil and change. Attuning to the meaning of this time and the messages from the Earth and sky allows us to open to the new consciousness and ways of being that we are being called into in our human evolution. It also allows us to more consciously let go of old patterns, forms, and ways of knowing. Rather than attaching to these old forms and resisting the change, we can honor the ending of what has been and open to what is being born.

To do this, we can engage in individual and community rites of passage. In ceremonies, we can symbolically let go of what needs to be released and honor what is dying or changing in our lives. We can do this through ceremonies with any of the elements (fire, water, earth, and air). With fire, we are able to burn what is being released, or with water, we can allow it to dissolve. Using the element earth, we may bury that which we are leaving behind. Utilizing meditation practices working with the breath, with our inhalation, we can take in the new ways of being and release the old patterns with the exhalation. Being in relationship with nature can teach us how to move with this life/death/rebirth cycle and to see it as a process of transformation. In letting go of our linear ways of knowing and returning to an understanding that nature operates in a cyclical or spiral manner, we can trust in these currents of change.

Engaging in a rite of passage also means holding and honoring the liminal time, the transition time when we feel that intense sense of vulnerability and insecurity as we have experienced the loss of who we were but do not yet know the new identity or new ways of being. Engaging in individual or group ceremonies to hold this transition in a sacred way is very important in order to stay centered emotionally, physically, and spiritually. Using ways of entering into altered states of consciousness (such as meditation, prayer, drumming, or chanting) allows us to seek guidance for the next steps in the change process and helps us to seek protection and solace in the times of uncertainty and existential anxiety.

In the transition time, there is often an impulse to seek answers and clarity from outside ourselves through a teacher, a group, or an institution that claims to provide the certainty that we seek. Teachers are helpful guides in the evolution of our consciousness; however, we need to be careful not to give over our power to another. This is the shadow side of the Age of Pisces and can lead to fanaticism and loss of the sense of self, not to union with spirit but to passivity and to yielding control to an idealized leader or group or belief system that gives us that illusion of certainty.

The challenge in the Age of Aquarius is to understand the deeper call to diversity and to equality and to step fully into our own connection with the Divine. In doing so, we realize that the energy of life, of spirit, is in all things. In that larger sense of interconnectedness, we recover a sense of our true identity as part of a larger whole. As we lose the illusion of individuality, we retain our own unique consciousness and experience of being one strand in the larger web of life. In finding our place in this larger whole, we can experience a deep sense of unity, community, and oneness while celebrating our own place. Like a drop in the sea, we can feel the wind and currents and move freely while knowing that we are ultimately merged with the larger cosmic ocean around us and within us.

In this time of change, we are moving out of the Kali Yuga (also known as the Age of Ignorance, when humans lose the wisdom that they once had known) and into the Dvapara Yuga, a time of increased awareness and enlightenment. In the Hindu understanding of these epochs, the times of decline for our human species are associated with periods when male power assumes dominance. It is significant that it has been in the time of patriarchy, across the past five thousand years, that we have experienced the destructive consequences of dualism and polarization in the separation of Earth and Sky, of male from female, and of humanity from nature and from our once unbroken communion with the spirit. Perhaps we needed to go through a developmental period of separation and individuation, much like the adolescent process, in order to further define and develop parts of ourselves neurologically, spiritually, and psychologically. However, to become mired in the false sense of separation can only lead to distortion and destruction, of ourselves and of the natural world in which we live.

Part of the challenge of this time is to honor the learning, the development that has occurred in these past ages. We have developed our left-brain capacities and learned how to experience the extent of our individual expression and creativity, but now we need to reintegrate those with a more balanced and whole sense of ourselves as part of the web of life. This time of transition is a time of moving beyond a belief system based on polarities to a time of unity consciousness. In modern physics, we now realize that the notions of self and other or self and a separate object of study are illusions. Everything is interconnected. However, we can reclaim that consciousness of interconnection while integrating the self-consciousness that we have fostered and developed across the past five thousand years. Rather than using that self-awareness for a false sense of separateness, control and exploitation, we can now use it to honor our relationship with all of life and to celebrate that larger unity. In returning to that natural sense of right relationship, we are able to truly honor the lives of the creatures around us and the natural resources of our world, not from a place of fear or of desperation, but from an attitude of reverence and love, realizing that we are indeed one.

CHAPTER TWELVE

SEEKING GUIDANCE FOR THIS TIME OF CHANGE

What guidance do we have to assist us in this time of change? In recent history, several outer planets have been discovered or rediscovered, in that there is evidence that ancient cultures were aware of these planets. The timing of their reemergence into our awareness has coincided with significant shifts in our collective consciousness associated with the archetypal meanings of the planets. Uranus, with its archetypal energy of creativity and radical change, was discovered in 1781 during the time of the American and French Revolutions. Interestingly enough, this time also coincides with the shift into the Hindu epoch the Dvapara Yuga of increased spiritual and intellectual awareness and enlightenment.

Neptune, with its message of dissolution of the self and of mysticism, was first observed by astronomers in 1846 at the time when the spiritualist movements were starting in the United States and in Europe and when the use of hypnosis and mesmerism became more prominent. In 1930, Pluto, the planet of profound transformation (of life/death/rebirth) came into our consciousness as the world was undergoing the global turmoil following World War I and preceding World War II with the concomitant massive global economic, political, and cultural changes. In addition, this was the period during which depth psychology and the understanding of the unconscious (individually and collectively) emerged.

These planets, in coming into our awareness, were bringing to human consciousness certain archetypal energies needed to guide us in the changes of those times. In consciously working with their meaning rather than resisting them, we further our own development and the evolution of our consciousness. Now, in this profound time of change, a new planet has been identified. This planet or planetoid, Sedna, has been named after the Inuit goddess of the deep sea. In exploring the nature of this newly discovered planetary body and the meaning of the myth that she has been named after, perhaps we can find wisdom for who we are and who we are being called to become in this intense time of transformation.

CHAPTER THIRTEEN

SEDNA: THE NEWLY DISCOVERED PLANETOID AND THE INUIT GODDESS OF THE SEA

In November 2003, astronomers from California's Mount Palomar Observatory discovered a planet deep in space and named her "Sedna" after the Inuit goddess of the sea due to her location in the dark, cold reaches of outer space. In the recent meeting of the International Astronomical Union (IAU) (in 2006), there was intense debate as to whether Sedna, Pluto and the newly discovered planetary body Xena (now "Eris") would be classified as planets or not. The result was that all were designated as dwarf planets or planetoids, although there is ongoing conflict in the astronomical community about this decision. Whatever the designation, it is significant that Sedna has been discovered and has brought the meaning of this Inuit goddess into the forefront of our consciousness.

Sedna, the planet or planetoid, is approximately three-fourths the size of Pluto and is so far from the Sun that, from her surface, you could block out the Sun with the head of a pin, according to astronomer Dr. Michael Brown. Sedna consists of ice and rock and is reddish in color. After Mars, it is the second reddest object in the solar system according to NASA (see the nasa.gov March 15, 2004 article "Planet-like Body Discovered at Fringes of Our Solar System"). Sedna is eight billion miles away and is the first object of the inner Oort cloud to be observed by astronomers. The Oort cloud circles the outermost edge of our solar system and consists of the repository of materials that supply the comets that enter our solar system and streak by the Earth. This debris consists of the remnants of the original nebula that collapsed and formed the Sun and all of the planets of our solar system five billion years ago. It is thought that the gravitational pull of Jupiter and other gas giants tends to keep this debris in the outer reaches of our solar system and cause the cometary material to be scattered into a spherical "cloud" surrounding our solar system. This Oort cloud is also affected by gravitational interaction with other star systems and sometimes overlaps with the Oort clouds of two other nearby stars.

Sedna has a very unusual elliptical orbit. The researchers who hypothesize that we are part of a binary star system believe that Sedna's unique elliptical orbit relates to the gravitational forces of our binary star. If so, then her coming into our consciousness at this time may also be as a messenger about the true nature of our solar system.

Sedna comes from the far reaches of our solar system, where it is so cold that the temperatures never rise above minus four hundred degrees Fahrenheit. This is one of the reasons that she was named after the Inuit goddess of the deep, frigid Arctic Sea. Sedna then travels in to circle our inner solar system before journeying out again to the outer edges of our system. She was observed in 2003 as she came close to our Earth. She will reach her closest approach to us in seventy-two years and then begin her journey back out into space. To complete one full orbit takes approximately 11,487 years. This means that the last time that Sedna was in her current position was at the end of the last ice age on Earth. It also means that her orbit is equivalent to almost half of the period of the precessional cycle.

What meaning does this planet hold for us? What wisdom does she bring to us from the outer reaches of our solar system, from the primordial matter of our origins? What does her namesake, the Inuit goddess of the sea, have to tell us about ourselves and this time?

To explore these questions, we must first listen to the story of Sedna, goddess of the deep sea. There are many versions of this Inuit myth. Here is a compilation and synthesis of some of the best-known versions:

The Tale of Sedna

Once upon a time there was a young Inuit woman named Sedna. She lived in the far north of Canada and was a rebellious young woman. Her family wanted her to marry to help hunt and fish and provide food for the family. Her father brought many men from the surrounding villages for her to choose a mate, but Sedna refused them all.

One day, a mysterious stranger walked into the village. He wore a long, black cloak with a hood pulled up over his head. Without knowing why, Sedna felt a stirring within her. She found herself drawn to him. When he asked her to go with him in his boat, she consented. Together, they left the village and journeyed far, far away to a barren island out in the sea. After they landed on the rocky shore, the mysterious stranger pulled back his hood, and Sedna gasped and saw that he was Raven. With fear and trembling, she knew that she was in the hands of the Magician, the Shaman, who knows the ways of the spirit world. Day after day, month after month, she struggled through the cold weather, the icy winds and the loss of all that she had left behind. There was not much to eat other than the few fish Raven brought back from his hunting. But all the while, Raven taught Sedna the ways of spirit.

After much time had passed, the villagers grew worried for her, not understanding where she had gone and why she never came back to visit her family and her village. Her father became afraid and decided that he must go and rescue her from her fate. He paddled his kayak out to her island. When he arrived, Raven was off hunting for fish, and Sedna sat alone on the shore. Seeing her on this cold, barren island, her father insisted on bringing her home with him. He pulled her toward his boat. "No, Father, I can not go home," Sedna replied. Her father would not listen to her words and carried her into his boat. He paddled rapidly out to sea, heading toward his village. Raven, returning from his hunt, realized that Sedna was gone. He cawed in rage and flew high over the sea to find her. Raven circled over the waves and saw Sedna in the boat with her father. Summoning the spirit of the wind and of the storm, Raven dove down by the boat and touched the tip of his wing to an ocean wave. The wind grew wild, and stormy waves rose and began to break over the sides of the boat.

Sedna's father, seeing that it was Raven, became filled with terror. He knew the power of Raven, and he felt the strength of the storm. Fearing for his life, he cried out to Raven, "Take her. Take Sedna. She's yours. Just spare me my life." And he threw his daughter overboard into the stormy sea. Sedna screamed and called out to her father, but to no avail. Frightened, she grabbed the side of the boat, trying to pull herself to safety. Her father took his paddle and hit her hands to keep her from getting back into the boat. Filled with anger and disbelief, Sedna again reached for the edge of the boat. Again and again, her father struck her fingers, until they broke off and sunk slowly beneath the surface of the sea. Sedna looked down and saw that her fingers had turned into seals and whales and dolphins, swimming off beneath the storm-tossed waves. Slowly, Sedna sank into the sea. Deeper, deeper she went, and the sea became quiet and dark and still. She began to feel her body dissolve. No longer bound by bones and skin, she felt herself become fluid, moving with the currents of the deep arctic waters. She felt one with the sea, and the sea became one with her. Looking around her, she saw whales and dolphins and seals calling out to her, calling her by name. And Sedna, the maiden was no more, and Sedna knew the magic and wisdom of the deep, and Sedna became the goddess of the sea.

Now, when people from the village set out to fish, they call to Sedna to honor her and ask her for protection. Hunters have great respect for her. Fishermen pour fresh water into the first catch of the day and thank Sedna for gifting the village with food to eat. They realize that as Raven knows the ways of the winds and the magic of the Earth and sky, Sedna knows the ways of the deep, dark sea. She is the goddess who can provide them with food and life, and the goddess who brings storms that can destroy them. To honor and appease her, shamans must swim down to her to comb her long, tangled hair and plead for the people. They understand that Sedna holds the power of life and death.

This story comes from the Inuit people, who live in the Arctic. The Arctic region extends from eastern Siberia to Greenland and is north of the tree line. The area consists of high mountains, sedimentary plains, bedrock, and lowlands with little or no soil. Because of the lack of soil, there are few edible plants. It is a cold and harsh environment with long, cold winters and short, cool summers as well as large seasonal shifts in sunlight. During the winter months, there is little sunlight, while in the summer, there are only a few hours of darkness. Year-round, the ground is frozen. During the winters, many of the channels of the Canadian Arctic Archipelago freeze.

Archeological evidence indicates that this region has been occupied by humans since about 10,000 BCE, about the time that the planetoid Sedna was in the position that it is in today in her orbit, in close proximity to our inner solar system. The Inuit people are more recent inhabitants in the Arctic and are distinct from other native populations in the area, according to anthropologists and linguists. They are descendants of the Thule people, who migrated from Asia about four and a half thousand years ago. The Inuit are a Mongol-type people and their name literally means, "the living ones who are here" (Qitsualik, *Nunatsiaq News*, June 27, 2003).

Due to the harsh environment, historically, the Inuit were a nomadic people who relied heavily on animal resources for their survival. They developed snow houses, harpoons and various types of boats and dogsleds to live and hunt for food. They relied on hunting land animals such as caribou, musk oxen, arctic foxes, and hares for food, and they were heavily dependent on marine life, including seals, walruses, whales, polar bears and arctic char.

"Sedna" is an English translation of the Inuit word "Siarnaq," the goddess of the sea, whose body parts gave birth to the sea creatures. She is also known among the Inuit people as "Talilajuk" and "Nuliajuk" (Qitsualik, *Nunatsiaq News*, March 19, 2004). She is the creation goddess on whom the people depended for food and for their survival.

There are many versions of the myth. Almost all of the stories hold the theme of Sedna's betrayal by her father and the people of her village, and the Inuit believed that Sedna not only was the source of their sustenance but also was the source of storms and of the harsh weather that could lead to their destruction. Therefore, the shamans' task was to appease Sedna, to dive into the depths of the sea to comb her hair and ask for her help in providing food for the people.

This story holds many layers of meaning for us in this time. On one level, it is the story of spiritual initiation. Sedna found herself drawn to the mysterious stranger and chose to follow him, even though this meant leaving behind her village and all that was familiar to her. Similar to Inanna's descent to the underworld, the journey did not unfold as Sedna might have expected. She found herself on a desolate island with Raven, the powerful teacher and shaman. While her journey was initiated by her will and her own intentions, she soon found herself in a situation beyond her control. All of what gave her a sense of identity and community had been stripped away, and she was alone with Raven in a harsh environment. For the Inuit people, isolation from the community often meant death. Those who became shamans had to face death and go off alone for a period of time for their initiation.

Like Sedna in the myth, we are now in a time of transition, leaving behind the familiar forms of our cultural heritage and moving into the wilderness of the unknown. In a parallel manner, this is part of our spiritual initiation and movement into a new level of consciousness.

While Sedna chose to leave her village and move into a new way of being, those who were part of her family and community were frightened by her departure and sought to rescue her. Sedna's father set out to find his lost daughter. Once he found her, he was angry and distraught to see her condition and that she was isolated on the barren island with Raven. He wanted to bring her back to the village, to her old way of life; however, once a journey of spiritual initiation has been undertaken, it can not be reversed. Sedna was in that liminal space between the worlds and was unable to go back to her life as she had known it.

Raven, the shaman and teacher, stirred up a terrible storm to prevent the father from taking Sedna away. Sedna's father, in his fear, betrayed Sedna and chose to sacrifice her life to save his own. He threw her overboard and then actively blocked her efforts to climb back into the boat by literally cutting off the fingers of her hands. Sedna died, sinking into the sea, with the bitter anger and sadness of this betrayal going with her. As she died, her body parts became whales and seals and the creatures of the sea. Sedna transformed, moving through this death/rebirth experience, and became the goddess of the sea, who held the power of life and death. The people feared her desire for revenge and worked to appease her as well as giving her gratitude for providing food from the sea. In this way, the story of Sedna restores the unity of the goddess archetype as the creator and destroyer, the one who brings both life and death.

Sedna speaks to the meaning of the time that we live in, when the familiar structures and forms that we have known culturally are in transition. Her story reminds us of the shadow side of the patriarchal era and the way in which we have been betrayed by the "fathers." In the story, the father's intentions were good; he set out to save his daughter and to protect his village. Yet, as we see with the shadow side of the sub-age of Virgo in the end of this Piscean Age, the effort for control often results in disconnection and destruction. In his desperation to survive and to cling to the way of life he had known, the father resisted the transformation that Sedna was undergoing and then tried to destroy her to save himself. Does this not resonate with some of the actions of our leaders in recent years, who, for example, have used "preemptive strikes" to preserve and protect themselves and their people? Today, we see many in positions of political and economic power who are struggling to cling to their power, control, and way of life through violence and by seizing others' lands and resources.

Sedna reminds us that sometimes we need to let go of everything and leave all that we have known behind, even though we have no idea where this journey may lead us. She also teaches us that the path of spirit means the loss of our ego identity and the dissolution of our sense of self. We need to dissolve and become part of the larger whole, at one with the sea and the cosmos. It is in this unity that we find our deeper purpose and meaning as part of the larger web of life.

In the story of Sedna, we understand the sea as the source of life and sustenance as well as the source of the storms that threaten our existence. Interestingly, a key archetypal theme in the Age of Pisces is the lineage of flood stories in which the sea rises and destroys the land and people. Neptune, the modern planetary ruler of the Age of Pisces, is associated with the "god of the sea," but as Liz Greene asserts, although it is named after a male Roman god, Neptune's deeper archetypal meaning is very much that of the "sea goddess" (Greene, *The Astrological Neptune and the Quest for Redemption*, p. xiv). In its deeper meaning, Neptune reminds us of the oceans, which are the source of all life on earth and the liquid womb from which we emerge at birth. The sea is the source of creation and destruction, our beginning and our end. In the flood myths that come from around the world and trace back into prehistory, the rising of the seas is often the way in which the gods cleanse the Earth of human wrongdoing or insolence. In the Judaic-Christian story of Noah, God sends the flood to punish the sinfulness of humanity. Noah is spared because of his righteousness and told to build an ark, which allows him to save himself and the seeds of plants and pairs of animals to repopulate the world.

The Hebrew story of Noah is a retelling of a more ancient Sumerian-Babylonian version. This was the story of Utnampishtim (mentioned earlier in reference to the epic of Gilgamesh) who was spared when Enki warned him of the impending flood and instructed him to build an ark. In all of these stories, the flood involves a cleansing of the Earth due to the conflicts between the realm of the Divine and humanity. In the Hebraic version, the flood is sent due to the sinfulness of humans, beginning with the "fall" when Adam and Eve went against God's injunction not to eat of the fruit of the Tree of the Knowledge of Good and Evil. In their action, they asserted their independence and gained consciousness but also experienced the rupture from blissful union with the Divine. These themes speak to the archetypal energies of separation and individuation in the Age of Aries and the longing during the Age of Pisces for redemption and reunion with the Divine.

Interestingly, in the earlier Sumerian-Babylonian version of this myth, the "original sin" is not an act of independence or defiance but rather one of blind obedience. In this story, Adapa, the son of Enki, angers the gods when he breaks the wing of the South Wind in a fit of anger. When Anu, the god of heaven, sends for Adapa to reproach him, Enki counsels his son to present himself in a penitent manner. He further instructs his son to refuse when Anu offers him the bread and water of death. Adapa follows his father's advice and comes to Anu in mourning and penance. Anu is pleased by his humility and piety and then offers him the bread and water of life, of immortality. In blind obedience to his father's instructions, Adapa misunderstands the offering and refuses it. In this way, he loses immortality, and the world is thereafter plagued with misfortune, disease and death as a result (see Greene, *The Astrological Neptune and the Quest for Redemption*, pp. 37-

38). These are perhaps the twin shadow sides of Neptune and the Age of Pisces, blind allegiance to an idealized other or fierce assertion of separation and individuation. Both result from the illusion of separation and the dilemma of dualism, whether it is the dualism of self and other, spirit and matter, or human and Divine.

The flood then becomes the dissolution of the false dualism, bringing us back to connection with source and to unity consciousness. In these ancient stories that surface throughout the world, often one of the gods (usually male) gives warning to the righteous human (in these stories, a man) and instructs him to build an ark for protection. In the myths, salvation comes through knowledge (the instructions from the Divine) and transcendence, through finding a way to rise above the floods of chaos and dissolution. The god provides the human with a path for control, for the ability to avoid the loss of self, of ego, and of life that comes with the rising waters. This too is a theme, especially of the final thousand years of the Age of Pisces. Since the Age of Reason, we see our desperate and ultimately destructive efforts to control the world around us, to manage the forces of nature and of our bodies in our effort to seek dominance and transcendence, and also, perhaps unconsciously, to gain divinity and immortality.

With the arrival of Sedna in our consciousness and the archetypal meaning arising from the Inuit myth, we have a very different version of the encounter with the oceanic waters, with the powers of the sacred feminine, the creatrix and destroyer. While the father in the story attempts to control the fate of himself and his daughter, again through the vehicle of a boat that rides above the waters, Sedna finds herself drowning and dissolving in the waters. The immersion in the waters of the ocean is not retribution or punishment for wrongdoing but rather a path for transformation and reunion with the Divine. The story reminds us that the way to divinity and unity is not through transcendence or control but rather through the dissolution of the ego and of the sense of separation.

While merging with the sea, with source, Sedna does not lose her awareness or consciousness. Instead, her form, her way of being, becomes fluid, no longer fixed or separate from source or from other life forms. She is now one with the sea but also with the creatures of the deep, the seals and whales and fish. She becomes a source of sustenance for the people, an ambassador of the ocean-mother-source while retaining her memory of her humanity. Sedna teaches us that we are not separate from the Divine, but that the Divine flows within and through us. She teaches us not to strive to deny our humanity or mortality but rather to dissolve into the deeper awareness of our ultimate nature, our union with source and with all of life.

This story speaks to our need in this time to no longer attempt to dominate or control nature or our life experience. Instead, we are asked to dive into the mystery, into the unknown, in trust that this transformation will lead to a more fluid, integrated, and whole way of being. This is the dissolution of the primary dualism that has characterized human consciousness for the past five thousand years and which is ultimately an illusion. This was also the message of Neptune in the Age of Pisces, that the very cause of our longing, our sense of separation, is ultimately an illusion, a false premise. The shattering truth of the Age of Aquarius and the lightning bolt awareness of Uranus is that all is one, all is energy. Form is merely a momentary manifestation of being, not a fixed reality.

With this awareness that Sedna brings to us in this time, perhaps then we can understand the deeper integration of Uranus and Saturn as the rulers of this Age of Aquarius. Within Western astrology, Uranus and Saturn (or Neptune and Saturn) have often been viewed as diametrically opposed in their meanings and intentions. Uranus is the energy of the reformer, the one who challenges cultural structures and norms. Saturn has been seen as the manifestation and enforcer of the societal structures and ideology. Saturn, as the outermost visible planet, has been viewed as the boundary between the infinite and the finite, between spirit and matter.

For the Greeks, Saturn was identified with Kronos, the father of time, binding us in our mortality and physical form. In medieval times, Saturn was seen as malefic, associated with age, illness, melancholy, and isolation. The planet was associated with the metal lead, at the opposite end of the spectrum for the alchemists from the lightness and purity of gold. As the split between spirit and matter became a primary duality in patriarchal thought, Saturn represented the fall from grace, from immortality and the purity of spirit unencumbered by form, into mortality and the constraints and entrapment of physical matter. In modern Western astrology, Saturn has been associated with our fears, restrictions and pain. Yet, the understanding has also been that if we work through these Saturnian issues, this planet leads us to deeper strength and wisdom.

Perhaps instead of this patriarchal understanding of Saturn, colored by the dualism between spirit and matter, we might look to an earlier archetype from the mythology of ancient Sumer and Babylon. In Babylonian mythology, Saturn was associated with "Ninurta" and was seen as sacred because this was the god closest to the sacred heavens. Ninurta was the god of agriculture, of the plow, and of thunderstorms. Ninurta gained power after rescuing the tablets of fate stolen from Enlil by the wind dragon in league with the powers of chaos. Here we see the way in which Saturn was elevated for its closeness to the sacred heavens and was viewed as the portal, bridging the worlds and opening us to our connection with the Divine. Ninurta was also the overseer of fate.

An even more ancient mythological reference for Saturn might be Enki, the Sumerian god of wisdom, the androgynous deity who rescued Inanna, the queen of heaven, from death, and the one who brought the knowledge of the ways of civilization (the sacred "me") to the people. Enki held the wisdom of how to move between the worlds, between the realm of the heavens and Earth as well as being the one who knew the way of descent and return from the underworld. In the Sumerian language, "Enki" means "god of the Earth" (Wolkstein and Kramer, *Inanna: Queen of Heaven and Earth,*, p. 146), yet he was also known as the god of the waters, fertilizing the Earth, bringing life and creativity.

While the realm of the heavens and Earth were split apart in the Sumerian cosmology at the threshold of the patriarchal period, Enki belonged to no realm; he moved between the worlds. In Sumerian mythology, he was the creator of humankind, the fertilizer of the land and the organizer of his creations (Wolkstein and Kramer, p. 147). He was the shaman, the magician, and the one who knew the ways of the universe and how to live an embodied life on Earth.

Enki's more fluid way of being and identity as the mediator between the realm of heaven and Earth and between the gods and humans is more consistent with the astronomical nature of the planet Saturn. This planet bridges the realm of the invisible and visible for us, as it is the outermost visible planet in our sky. Yet unlike its medieval associations with lead and the weight of form, it is a gaseous planet and the only one in our solar system that is less dense than water. It is almost entirely gas and liquid and consists mostly of hydrogen, the life force of the universe. Astronomers now question whether it has a solid rock core or, more likely, a molten/liquid core. In its essence, Saturn is fluid and bridges the worlds. Saturn has a hot interior and radiates more energy into space than it receives from the Sun. It is surrounded by beautiful rings of ice and space debris, which it has shaped into form with its gravitational field. These ever-changing rings speak to us of the possibilities of living in a more fluid and ever-changing manner.

We are now in a time when we must face the challenge of integrating spirit and matter and no longer live in the destructive illusion of duality. We need to move into a new cosmology in which we realize that there is no separation between Earth and sky, flesh and spirit. As hydrogen moves through the universe as a river of energy, fueling the stars and planets, so spirit moves through all of life. Like Enki and Saturn, when we are embodied, our form is not fixed. We do not belong to one realm or the other. We are fluid, like Sedna, manifesting for this moment in this shape and incarnation, which rather than being a separation from spirit, is a celebration of spirit's endless possibilities of manifestation. Unless we truly embrace this awareness and let go of the illusion of separation and dualism, we are destined to engage in an endless struggle between our spiritual and natural selves and between ourselves and the Earth, the planet where we reside.

In this way, we now may view the planetary rulers of this new Age of Aquarius, Saturn and Uranus, not as antagonists but as allies. Uranus shatters the illusions, the forms that bind us from our true essence, and it reminds us of our essential, energetic being. Saturn allows us to find the ways to integrate that awareness and essence in form, holding the manifestation lightly, knowing that it is fluid and never fixed. This is the shamanic understanding of shape-shifting, the wisdom that all is spirit, all is energy; we can partake of form in celebration rather than in confinement, be open to change, and live in the enormity of the possibilities of the universe. If we could but embrace that truth, that consciousness, the world could transform in the blink of an eye.

CHAPTER FOURTEEN

OUR NEW "DWARF" PLANET ERIS, OR XENA

Another guide to us in this time of change is the newly discovered planet (now demoted to dwarf planet) Eris, or Xena. Discovered in 2005 (from images taken in 2003) by astronomers Michael Brown (Caltech), Chad Trujillo (Gemini Observatory) and David Rabinowitz (Yale University), she is the largest dwarf planet known (see Tindol, "The Dwarf Planet Formerly Known as Xena Has Officially Been Named Eris, IAU Announces"). When the planet was first identified, the discoverers and NASA declared her to be our solar system's tenth planet due to her size (which has been determined to be about four percent larger than that of Pluto). Eris is a trans-Neptunian body orbiting the Sun just beyond the Kuiper belt. This belt consists of asteroids and cometary matter scattered outward in our solar system beyond the orbits of the planets. Sedna, whose orbit is much larger than that of Eris, is another of these trans-Neptunian objects (TNOs), but her orbit extends out even further than Eris and interfaces with the Oort cloud, the outermost cometary matter in our solar system.

What is unique about Eris is that her orbit is eccentric and very different from those of the other planets in our solar system; her orbit is tilted off the path of the ecliptic by forty-four degrees. This is why she was not discovered until 2003, when astronomers began to search the sky beyond the path of the ecliptic. It takes 556.7 years for her to complete an orbit, and she is now at her farthest distance from the Sun (almost ten billion miles, even farther out than Sedna at this time and three times more distant than Pluto). She currently is moving through the constellation Cetus. She was in Sculptor until 1929 and will now be in Cetus until she enters Pisces in 2036. She rarely moves through the constellations of our zodiac, due to her highly inclined orbit.

In the August 2006 meeting of the International Astronomical Union, her discovery generated debate as to whether she should be classified as a planet or not. In the ensuing conflict among the astronomers, she was designated as a dwarf planet, and Pluto was demoted to this status as well, along with Ceres. Due to her size and those of Pluto and Ceres, either all three had to be classified as planets or they had to be designated as dwarf planets. In the contentious debate, the resulting definition of a planet was that it was necessary for the planetary body to be in orbit around the Sun, to have sufficient mass so as to be nearly round in shape and to have "cleared the neighborhood around its orbit." It is this last qualification that excluded Pluto, Ceres and Eris from planetary status due to the fact that all of them share their orbits with those of other planetary bodies. Pluto shares its orbit with its large moon, Charon, and its orbit intersects with the orbit of Neptune for part of the time. Interestingly, this requirement did not exclude Neptune from planetary status. Ceres and Eris share space with surrounding asteroid belts and do not "clear their orbits" and become the primary entity in their orbital field; instead, they are in essence part of a larger community.

From a philosophical perspective, this newly formed definition of a planet by the IAU is significant. In essence, it creates a definition of importance that is defined by isolation and individualism. To be a planet, it is important to be large and to so dominate your own field of movement that you are the only primary body in that area of space. Pluto is in essence a double planet, with its moon Charon almost its same size, and it is able to move in and out of orbit with Neptune. Ceres is part of the main asteroid belt between Mars and Jupiter, while Eris is among the Kuiper belt asteroids. Sedna also is a Kuiper belt object, and its orbit intersects with the inner Oort cloud. These planetary bodies perhaps bring into our collective consciousness a corrective to the idealization of individuation and a new perspective about connection and community. It is interesting that these planets, or planetoids, are calling us out of our overemphasis on individualism and isolationism at the same time that we are rediscovering that our solar system may be part of a binary star system and as we move into the Age of Aquarius with its emphasis on community.

The contentious debate and ongoing conflicts about this new definition of a planet and the resulting designations led the astronomers of the IAU to the name the planetoid Eris after the Greek goddess of strife, and Eris's moon was named Dysnomia, the demonness of lawlessness and one of the Greek goddess's children. Eris is most well known in Greek mythology for her role in triggering the Trojan War by stirring up conflict among the Olympian goddesses. When she was not invited to a wedding party, Eris arrived unannounced and tossed a golden apple into the crowd, which read "Kallisti," meaning "for the fairest one." This action resulted in the goddesses Hera, Athena and Aphrodite all vying for the prize, with each trying to bribe the judge, Paris, the prince of Troy, who was chosen by Zeus to resolve the conflict. When Paris was offered Helen, wife of Sparta, by Aphrodite if she was chosen, Paris consented. This sequence of events led to the Trojan War and resulted in the destruction of the city of Troy. This tale shows the dangers of competition, abuse of power, and strife. In the end, the need to be the best, the one chosen from the field of competitors, led to the downfall of all involved.

In selecting this name for this new planetary body, the IAU may have consciously or unconsciously signaled its own shortsightedness. The effort to restrict the definition of a planet was an effort to cling to the chosen few who have "cleared their neighborhoods" and seemingly shown their power and prowess in the process. The astronomers themselves, in their need to avoid the expanding community of planets that would result from a more liberal definition, may have set themselves up for ongoing strife, competition, and conflict.

In contrast, let us consider what we know of the nature of this new planetary body, which for two years prior to this debate was known as "Xena." Astronomer Michael Brown, a fan of the popular television series (September 1995–May 2001) *Xena: Warrior Princess*, named her after this heroine. He named her moon Gabrielle, for Xena's companion and closest friend. The setting for the television show was ancient Greece, and it drew liberally on ancient mythologies from around the world. The primary story line was about Xena's transformation from a violent warlord to a spiritual warrior on a quest for justice and healing for all.

Xena had initially become a warlord bent on revenge after being traumatized and enraged as a child watching her village being destroyed by warriors. After years of seeking revenge on those who had destroyed her village and family, she underwent a profound transformation, realizing that she had become the enemy that she hated. She then took a radically different path and set out on a quest to become a warrior for peace and justice, to right the wrongs of her previous crimes and to try to end the cycle of violence.

In the series, Xena moved through many adventures with other characters from assorted historical periods and cultures making their appearance on the show. Time, history, and culture were fluid as they wove through the narratives. The character Xena refused to ally with any group, though many tried to gain her allegiance. She was a warrior of the people, of those in need and those who were in danger or unjustly treated. She intervened to bring peace, life, and justice, and then she moved on. Her quest was not for fame, for power, or for material advantage but rather to set wrongs right. She moved through many relationships with friends and many sexual encounters including a brief erotic interlude with her female companion. Her sexuality was her own, and she engaged in a diversity of relationships, which are Aquarian traits.

At the end of the series, Xena's daughter, Eve, born out of wedlock, was decreed to be the one who would bring about the death of the Olympian gods. In an effort to thwart this prophecy, the gods attempted many preemptive strikes to kill Eve in order to retain their power. During this time, Xena and Gabrielle went through their own death/rebirth experience. After a period of twenty-five years, Eve accepted her purpose and her fate and stepped into her part in the profound transformation of the culture around her, leading to the end of the religion of that era.

The Olympian pantheon came into prominence in Greece at the end of the first millennium BCE and continued into the time of the Hellenistic period in the early centuries AD, at the beginning of the Age of Pisces. Xena, a character created in our culture at the end of the

Age of Pisces, was depicted in the storyline of the series as instrumental in the transition out of the earlier Age of Aries.

Our current Western civilizations have been profoundly shaped by Greek cosmology arising in the Age of Aries and, in particular, by the Platonic notion of the ideal as separate from material reality and reflecting the separation of spirit from matter. The ancient Greek culture also idealized the mental capacities and forms of logic which so permeate our Western ways of thinking and knowing. The character Xena, in her effort to set things back into balance, into right relationship, perhaps hints to us of a return to a more natural form of law and more integrated notion of spirit and matter.

Unlike Eris, Xena was dedicated to undoing the damage of strife and warfare. Perhaps even now, Xena teaches us how to follow her example and radically transform our lives and step out of the cultural patterns and collective consciousness of our time. Through her deep inner and outer exploration, Xena became aware of and freed herself from her unconscious reactivity and cultural conditioning and stepped into a new way of being at the threshold of a new age. She embarked on a journey with no clear destination, whose only purpose was to live in truth, to act from the heart, and to serve justice. Her companion in the series, Gabrielle, in contrast to Dysnomia, the demonness of lawlessness, was known for her sensitivity and compassion and her love of mythology and for the way in which stories weave meaning and connections in our lives.

The character of Xena is much more in attunement with this new planetary body, whose orbit is so eccentric and off the beaten path of the ecliptic than the name that the astronomical community assigned to her. Our recently discovered dwarf planet, like Xena, follows her own path, circling in close to the Sun and the other planets of our solar system and then off into the more outer edges of the Kuiper belt. She moves in harmony, not disharmony, with the other planetary bodies around her but dares to be unique in her orbit. She has no need to "clear her neighborhood" to prove her dominance or to strive for hierarchical advantage. She was content to move unseen in our midst for millennia and was not noticed until astronomers dared to look at the sky with a new perspective.

True to her original name, she shows us how to step out of our cultural conditioning and engrained patterns of thinking and acting. From an astrological perspective, she defies our efforts to place her on the ecliptic, because her very nature is about her disengagement from this "traditional" or normative path. At this time at the end of the Age of Pisces and the beginning of a new age, she teaches us how to change our lives and how to step out of old patterns and habitual ways of knowing, doing, and being. She asks us to dare to embark on a journey into the unknown and to live in right relationship with all of life around us.

How significant that this planetary body evoked conflict in the astronomical community and a subsequent effort to demote her from planetary status to a "dwarf planet" and to name her after the Greek goddess of strife. Perhaps this decision reflects our fear of or reaction to her unique character and her audacity in stepping off the ecliptic and out of a traditional orbit and way of being. Her original name, Xena, seems to correspond more closely with her true nature, and is it not significant that in this age of technology, one myth for our time may come from our modern media? In this time of transition and global change, the debate about Xena/Eris may reflect the tumult between the call to new forms of consciousness and new ways of being and the rigid, regressive efforts to cling to old forms and traditional beliefs.

The dwarf planet now travels through the constellation Cetus, one of the constellations (along with Aquarius, Pisces, and Eridanus) in the southern sky, in the region known as the Water. The ecliptic touches the edge of this constellation, but for the most part, Cetus lies below it and is associated in Greek mythology with the gateway to the underworld. Cetus in Greek and Roman mythology was seen as the whale, which reminds us of the mythology of Sedna, the goddess of the deep sea who has whales and seals as her companions. The Arabs, along with the ancient Hebrews and Greeks, viewed this constellation as a serpentine sea creature.

In Mesopotamia, the stars of Cetus were associated with Tiamat, the primordial mother of all life in Sumerian and Babylonian mythology. While imaged in modern interpretations as a "sea monster," Tiamat was not depicted this way in the ancient stories. Instead, she was associated with the deep sea, with the primordial waters from which all life comes.

She gave birth to the dragons and serpents, which we know were the earliest images of the sacred feminine and of the Divine, both in the sky and on Earth. She was the supreme goddess of the sea and of the source, the chaos of creation. In the Babylonian epic the Enuma Elish, she is the holder of the tablets of destiny who is later slain when the gods fear her powers of creation and destruction, and she is sliced in half to form the heavens and the Earth.

So our new planet, as she passes through this constellation, reminds us of the depths, of the source of all of life, of the power of chaos, the cauldron of creation and destruction. She heralds the return of the sacred feminine and the transformation and dissolution of our current patriarchal belief systems. She encourages us to let go of our personal stories and cultural conditioning and to dive deep and return to right relationship with source and with all of life.

CHAPTER FIFTEEN

AROUND THE WHEEL AND BACK TO CENTER

We have now journeyed through more than half of the wheel of the zodiac with the precession of astrological ages. We have seen how the archetypal themes of the constellations and their associated archetypes and mythologies shape our human and cultural experience when these stars touch our sky at the vernal equinox and how the movement of the stars is mirrored in our lives on Earth.

Interestingly, as we have followed this circuit from the Age of Leo to the Age of Aquarius, the rulers of these ages have moved from the innermost part of our solar system outward. The Age of Leo is ruled by the Sun, the star at the center of our solar system. Then, in order, moving through the zodiac, the rulers are the Moon (Age of Cancer), Mercury (Age of Gemini), Venus (Age of Taurus), and Mars (Age of Aries). In our most recent astrological ages, we have two co-rulers, one traditional and one modern to include the outer planets discovered in the past few centuries. So, for the Age of Pisces, we have Jupiter and Neptune as the rulers and then Saturn and Uranus for Aquarius. As can be seen, these rulers take us from the center of our solar system outward to the outer planets.

In astrology, the Sun, Moon and inner planets are viewed as shaping our personal lives, while the outer planets (Uranus, Neptune, and Pluto) are transpersonal planets, which affect the themes of our generational periods and guide us to seek a larger meaning and purpose for our lives. These planets are beyond our vision and move in slower cycles, exerting their influence on us over longer periods of time. Dane Rudhyar, one of the foremost Western astrologers and philosophers, describes these outer planets as vehicles of transformation, bringing us the wisdom of the spiritual realm beyond our personal and cultural ways of knowing and being (see Rudhyar, *The Galactic Dimension of Astrology: The Sun is Also a Star*, p. 87).

What is important to remember is that, while one aspect of the wheel may be more dominant in a certain age, we live in every moment within the wheel in its entirety. The archetypal themes and myths of the past ages are a part of our ancestral and incarnational lineage. They shape our lives in a very personal way as well as being a part of our history and cultural evolution. As the ancients knew, the path toward wholeness is to eventually step off the wheel and come to center, to integrate the meanings and wisdom of the whole rather than living out one part or aspect. As we are surrounded by all of the signs of the zodiac and the wisdom of all of the planetary rulers in our birth charts, so we live every day with the tapestry of stars encircling our Earth. Perhaps in this time of crisis globally and environmentally, it is more important than ever before that we find our way to the center, to integrate the wisdom of the stars and to find healing, wholeness, and right relationship with all of life.

Some astrologers speculate that because our Sun is now aligned with the galactic center at the winter solstice that we have come to the end of the Great Sidereal Year, the precessional cycle through all the signs of the zodiac, which is a twenty-six-thousand-year cycle. If this is the case, then we are indeed in a time of profound transition as we move into a new cycle and new era as well as a new astrological age.

Our awareness of Sedna also speaks to these larger cycles in that Sedna's orbit is 11,487 years. The last time that she was in the place in the sky where she is now was at the time of the ending of the last ice age, a time of enormous Earth changes. Graham Hancock, in his book *Underworld: The Mysterious Origins of Civilization*, has researched that period of time and describes the massive earthquakes, floods, and volcanic eruptions that occurred as the ice melted across the continents. He also conjectures that civilization as it was at that time disappeared as the advanced cultures residing along the coastlines were flooded with the rise in sea levels. The enormous upheaval and flooding of that time may have led to the worldwide myths about the Great Flood. Archeologists are now searching beneath the waters along the coasts of Mexico, India, and other countries for the remains of these lost civilizations.

Sedna returns again to our inner solar system in a time of global and environmental tumult. We are experiencing a record number of severe storms, hurricanes, tsunamis, earthquakes, and floods related to global warming and the effects of the melting of the ice cap in the Arctic and the glaciers in Antarctica. Until we wake up and remember that we are intimately connected with the land, sea, and air around us, these conditions will only worsen.

Perhaps our newly discovered planet, or planetoid Xena (Eris) is the guide, showing us how to access Sedna's message and wisdom. Xena demonstrates for us how to step off the ecliptic, out of our ingrained patterns of knowing and being, and how to move between the worlds. She helps us to let go of our personal and collective fixed beliefs and teaches us that we can in fact transform our lives. She shows us that we can move from a path of violence and domination to one of peace and right relationship. We can open to diversity, to the interconnectedness of all of life and live in a more present and fluid manner.

So, if the outer planets bring us transpersonal guidance, what is the core meaning and message of Sedna? Perhaps it could be said that her wisdom is of epochs, of larger cycles of our human evolution, and beyond that, she guides us to a galactic consciousness that takes us beyond our ego identities and even beyond our identification with the Earth and our solar system. With her vast orbit, bringing her into contact with the primordial matter of our universe, she is a messenger from the sky reminding us of our cosmic origins. Sedna speaks to us of the power of nature and of spirit, to birth us, nurture us and also to destroy us as well. She also shows us our place in the larger cosmos and teaches us humility. While we tend to focus on ourselves and our importance on the Earth and on our place in the inner solar system with the Sun as our center, Sedna reminds us that we are a part of a larger galaxy of star systems. She guides us to remember our source in the oceans of this planet and our source in the ocean of the sky above us. If we listen, she whispers to us to remember our birthplace in the cosmos, our true source and center.

CHAPTER SIXTEEN

FINDING OUR CENTER

So what is this birthplace, this source, the cosmic womb that has given birth to all life? Across the past century, physicists and astronomers have been struggling to grasp the nature of the energies of our universe and the nature of the galactic center. Their findings have revolutionized our understanding of reality. Einstein's explorations of the forces moving through the cosmos have led to the theory of relativity and the revision of Newtonian physics, which has shaped our understanding of the cosmos for the past five hundred years. Recent research with the use of the Hubble telescope and examinations of the galactic center through radio and gamma-ray technologies have led us to a deeper understanding of the nature of the center of our galaxy.

As we noted at the beginning of our journey through the zodiac, across human history, we have searched for the path to the center. The medicine wheel, the mandala, and the circle as symbols for wholeness and the search for source permeate all cultures and all religions. Ancient cultures oriented their land and located the seat of power and of sacred sites at the center of their region. We have searched for the center in the sky from the ancient focus on the celestial pole as a source of stillness in the swirling landscape of stars to the ancient cultural view of the Milky Way as the source of life where the World Tree attaches and holds the universe intact.

So where is the center that we can orient our lives from? As we look for the center, we first must honor our location on our Earth, our home. Then we journey out to the center of our solar system, our Sun. Then we remember that our Sun is one star among the three-hundred billion stars in our Milky Way galaxy and may be one in a binary star system revolving around a central point. Finally, we look to the center of our galaxy, our ultimate source. This is what Sedna is guiding us toward as she moves from the primordial matter of our solar system, the Oort cloud, experiences the energies of the surrounding star systems, and then brings that awareness back into our inner solar system.

Our Earth resides in the Milky Way galaxy, a spiral galaxy consisting of three-hundred billion stars and a diameter of about one hundred thousand light years. Our galaxy is the second largest in a group of over thirty galaxies that compose what is called the Local Group of galaxies (Melia, *The Black Hole at the Center of Our Galaxy*, p. 3). The nearest galaxy is Andromeda, which is 2.4 million light years away. Our solar system is on the Orion arm of our Milky Way galaxy about two-thirds of the way out or about thirty-thousand light years from the center. We orbit around this galactic center at about 250 kilometers per second, taking 220,000 years to complete one cycle. Our Sun was formed roughly 4.6 billion years ago, so the elements that make up our bodies have orbited the center of our galaxy approximately twenty times (Melia, p. 8).

Recent research has shown that we live in a universe of which only 4 percent is matter as we know it. Twenty-three percent is unseen dark matter, and 73 percent is dark energy, of which we only have the beginning glimmers of understanding. Of the 4 percent that is visible matter, astronomers have only seen and researched 1 percent of that. We live in a universe filled with mystery far beyond our comprehension and in a spiral galaxy filled with wonder.

What is the center of our galaxy? Only in recent years have scientists come to understand more fully the location and nature of our galactic center. Prior to the use of radio telescopes, our most powerful optic telescopes were unable to glimpse this amazing site due to the cloud of space dust obscuring our vision. Through radio astronomy, we are able to move beyond this veil to glimpse the amazing source of our galaxy. What we now know is that if the galactic center were unobscured, its size and brightness would be comparable to those of the full Moon, lighting up our night sky (Melia, p. 8). Instead, it moves in darkness, veiled from our eyes. Surrounding the galactic center is a concentration of stars, drawn by the powerful gravitational pull of this source. It is from this center that our galaxy was formed almost fourteen billion years ago in a cosmic explosion. As we noted earlier, this concentration of stars is viewed through our constellation Sagittarius, the archer, whose arrow points into the galactic center.

What is the nature of this cosmic source? Our radio telescope views of this amazing site have given us some sense of the composition of this region. What we find are a concentration of stars and three spiraling arms of hot gas, known as Sagittarius A West, emanating from the source and moving in a counterclockwise manner, a triskelion of sorts. There is also an enormous bubble of hot gas, known as Sagittarius A East, that is most likely the remains of a star that ventured too close to the center and exploded, yielding the power of fifty to one hundred supernovas (Melia, p. 15). At the center of all of this pulsing, moving heat and energy is Sagittarius A*, what we now know to be a massive black hole with the power of 2.6 million Suns emanating from its source and with a diameter about the size of the orbit of our planet Mars (Melia, p. 40). While stars close to this center move at amazing speeds (up to five million kilometers per hour), because of its phenomenal gravitational pull and the triple spiraling arms of hot gas that dance in graceful movement around it, Sagittarius A*, the galactic center, is the still point and source of our galaxy as it moves through the universe.

What is it made of? This super-massive black hole is composed of "dark" matter, meaning its gravitational pull is so great that it absorbs all matter and light. Physicists since Einstein and the theory of relativity have realized that gravity affects both light and time. Strong gravitational energy can bend light and slow down time. The compressed energy of the black hole at the center of our galaxy is so great that no light can escape from it, and time stops. It becomes a world unto itself from which nothing can escape, surrounded by a virtual membrane, the event horizon. This amazing center is the source of all of life in our galaxy and the place of its ending; it is the creatrix and the destroyer. It is the dark womb that has given birth to all of the stars in our galaxy and the tomb, drawing them in to die. Within this compressed source of power is a mystery beyond our wildest imagining and a realm that we can never fully comprehend. Brian Swimme refers to this amazing source as the "all-nourishing abyss," the "foundational reality of the universe" and the "ocean of potentiality" that brings forth all life and then absorbs it back into itself (Swimme, *The Hidden Heart of the Cosmos,* p. 100).

What is also amazing for us to comprehend is that we live in an expanding universe. Einstein's mathematical formulations, which shocked even him, indicate that the galaxies are moving away from each other at a velocities related to the space between them (Swimme, p. 75). In other words, the greater the distance between them, the faster they are moving apart. At the birth of our universe, there was an explosion that we can still monitor in terms of the movement of photons across the galaxies. Yet, amazingly, this fiery birth was also the beginning of our notions of space and time. There was no space or time before this creation. From the void, came all of life.

As Edwin Hubble discovered, as we measure the galactic expansion, we discover that we are at the center, with everything moving away from us. In other words, every point used to measure this expansion becomes the center. Brian Swimme, in *The Hidden Heart of the Cosmos,* explores this amazing paradox. What we find is that we live in a complex, omnicentric evolutionary universe, with a cosmic explosion as our birth - yet at the same time, a "developing reality which from the beginning is centered upon itself at each place of its existence" (Swimme, p. 85).

What does this discovery mean? It means that our former Newtonian notions of space and time were inaccurate and inadequate. For centuries, we have held a view of ourselves as fixed in space and time, consisting of solid form. We now know that concept is an illusion. We initially began to come to this awareness through the discovery that we consist of atoms – tiny, invisible molecules of matter, existing in an expanse of space. We are mostly space, the expansiveness between these molecules. Yet, now, our scientific understanding has taken us even deeper into the realization that even this conception is false. In reality, we now know that the elementary particles of life, photons, the light energy that forms into matter, arise out of the vacuum itself. They do not move in space or stay in a fixed state; they "foam" into and out of existence. Physicists refer to this ground of being as "space-time foam" (Swimme, p. 93). As Swimme describes it:

[The] elementary particles and atoms are not permanently existing objects but are events that are vibrating at extremely rapid rates. Even the word "vibrate" is not exact, for it connotes a solid object that moves rapidly back and forth in space… [We] know in fact that it is not true to think of particles moving back and forth in space. Rather, as has been celebrated and discussed throughout most of the twentieth century, particles exist in one location and then exist in another location *without traversing the space in between.* So, as bewildering as it might sound to us, it is more accurate, scientifically to say that the particles and atoms are flashing into existence, surging into existence, and then just as suddenly they are dissolving from their place to surge forth in a nearby location…

(Swimme, p. 102)

Beyond the reach of our eyes, and almost beyond the capabilities of our imagining, the particles of life foam into being and then dissolve again, everywhere throughout the universe. This birthing of our universe at the galactic center is thus mirrored throughout time and space. We and all of life arise out of the fecund void, the womb of the universe, the great goddess of creation and destruction and move through cycles of birth/death and rebirth. This galactic center is our birthplace, our true center, and yet the act of creation and the center is also within each of us at each moment. We dance into being and then dissolve back into the sea of all being, of all potentiality. With the galactic center, we are co-creators of our own destiny and move with the currents and rhythms of the Earth and the sky.

CHAPTER SEVENTEEN

PLUTO AT THE CENTER

The ancient art and science of astrology is a source of wisdom and guidance for our lives, individually and collectively, as we have seen in moving through the ages. The discoveries of the planets signal a new awareness emerging in our consciousness and guide us in our human evolution. If we tune in to the cycles of the planets, they also give us more detailed guidance for the phases and cycles of our lives, individually and generationally. As we have noted, the outer planets in particular bring us that transpersonal wisdom and guidance.

In light of this awareness, it should not surprise us to find that across the past twenty-five years, all three of the outer planets in our solar system have come into alignment with the galactic center. As was noted earlier, we find the galactic center, Sagittarius A*, located at three degrees of Sagittarius in the sidereal zodiac, or at twenty-six degrees Sagittarius in the tropical zodiac. First, Neptune moved back and forth over this point in the sky from February 1981 through October 1984 (given a two-degree orb). Then, from January 1987 to November 1988, Uranus was in alignment with the galactic center. Finally, Pluto came into alignment from December 2005 to October 2008.

In that we are still integrating the effects of these transits, it is not possible to fully or definitely formulate what these alignments mean for us. However, it is significant, given our movement through the zodiac and the astrological ages, that first, Neptune, the ruler of Pisces, came into alignment, and then Uranus, the ruler of Aquarius, and now

Pluto, the ruler of Sagittarius, the constellation that is the home of this galactic center.

If we view this period of time in our human history as a time of intensification and purification, a call to a radical shift in consciousness – as was stated in the ancient prophesies of the Mayans, Hopis, Hindus, and others – then it is truly a profound synchronicity that these outer planets have all come into alignment with the galactic center within the past two decades. Tuning back in to the core archetypal meanings of these outer planets, we might speculate that Neptune's alignment was calling on us to dissolve our attachments to our former ways of thinking and being and to release the themes of the Piscean Age. Uranus was channeling to us new ways of thinking and being based on our understanding of energy and cosmic unity and was calling us into a deeper understanding of our humanity and our divinity. In this way, Uranus was shattering our former ideologies and understandings and was creating the space for a new form of consciousness to emerge. Pluto, god of the underworld, of death and rebirth, was radically transforming us. Pluto called us to die to our past ways of life and to undergo a profound alchemical transformation, a radical rebirth, into a new consciousness and incarnation.

CHAPTER EIGHTEEN

CONCLUSION: COMING FULL CIRCLE

Now that we have moved around the wheel of the zodiac and found our way to the center, what does it all mean? How have this exploration of the sky and our ancient and modern understandings of it provided us with any guidance for our lives in this time? We have come to realize that the movements in the sky are mirrored in the events on the Earth and that we can find meaning in the stars and planets that surround us. We have searched for the center and found it in the heart of the galaxy and within ourselves. But what does this mean for our day-to-day lives?

In that we are in a profound time of transition – astrologically, globally, and environmentally – we need to realize that we are in a time of letting go and yet not knowing what new forms or ways of being will emerge. This situation is similar to the monthly lunar cycle, when at the time of the dark of the Moon, the old cycle has ended but the new Moon has not yet become visible in the sky. We now live in a time of mystery, in a liminal period, and we need to honor being in the dark, without knowing what will be born on the other side of this profound time of change. We know from ancient prophesies and modern science that this is a time of intense change and a time when either we need to change our ways of thinking and being or we are likely to self-destruct as a species. But what the change means, what we are meant to become, what the new forms of consciousness are; those things we can not fully know. So, part of the challenge of our time is to honor that process of releasing, of dying to what has been, without knowing the shape or form of what is to come.

This process of letting go and of honoring the liminal time (the in-between space) is a critical phase of any rite of passage, and this is the message of Neptune and of Sedna. Rather than fighting to cling to the past and to what is familiar, we need to let those old ways of being dissolve. This is the lesson of nonattachment and the ancient wisdom of dying to ourselves (and our former ways of being) that we might be reborn. We can honor this letting go through individual and group rituals and rites of passage. For example, we may want to ceremonially release those ways of being that no longer serve us by symbolically giving them to the sea or writing them down on paper and burning them in a fire.

We also can live that reality daily in breaking old habits and patterns that keep us locked in to an illusion of security and familiarity. This way of living does not mean becoming chaotic or impulsive in our behavior, but rather it means bringing that deeper galactic consciousness to our day-to-day lives in realizing that what we view as fixed and determined and stable in our lives is really an illusion. It is as if the forms and structures of our lives and of our world are fractals that have appeared from the sea of chaos and potentiality and must dissolve back into that source for some new form and structure to emerge. If we can view all of matter, systems, and structure in this way, we can live in a more fluid manner and not attach our identity or security to particular patterns, structures, or forms.

On a practical level, this means that we need to simplify our lives. In living more simply, we can begin to honor a more sustainable way of being. In decluttering our external environment, we can begin to attune to what is truly necessary and authentic to our lives at a deeper level. It is also important to reduce the clutter and chatter in our internal lives by taking time away from the overstimulation of the world around us so that we can meditate, listen to the wisdom within, and take time to listen and attune to the natural world again.

Being open to these changes also means being open to the unknown and to the new ways of being that will emerge. Culturally, it is as if we have only viewed reality as that 4 percent of visible matter in our universe. Yet, 96 percent of our universe is mysterious dark energy and unseen dark matter. We live in a reality that we cannot understand. Our lives are embedded in mystery. We float in a cosmic womb that holds us but is beyond our control or comprehension. As we realize that we are truly a part of our unfathomable universe and shaped by larger cosmic patterns and cycles, we can find our security in that mystery and in our awe of the source of our being.

It is an amazing synchronicity that 4 percent of the universe is visible matter, and scientists have discovered that only 4 percent of our DNA accounts for our visible form. The other 96 percent has been labeled "junk DNA" for DNA with no known function due to our blindness to what is beyond the visible realm (see the article by Dr. Susumu Ohno in the Brookhaven Symposium on Biology in 1972). Many spiritual teachers and shamans tell us that this remaining DNA is what holds the star wisdom and our connection to the wisdom from across time and space. By engaging in meditation, shamanic journeys or through experiences of altered consciousness, we can open to the wisdom within our bodies that connects us with the stars and with the matrix of creation and of the universe. Modern scientific knowledge, achieved through our observations, is only able to help us to access a limited amount of information, just as we have been able to actually observe and research only 1 percent of the universe (one-fourth of the visible matter). Utilizing more ancient and shamanic ways of knowing can allow us to more directly access wisdom and guidance from the universe. These more intuitive right-brain ways of knowing provide an important balance and complement to our left-brain analytical ways of learning.

In this time of profound change, we are opening more fully to the visible and invisible realms and are letting go of old belief systems and ways of being. The changes in the world around us call us into transition and transformation. We are bombarded daily by news of global chaos, terrorism, and war. We hear scientists talk of "peak oil" and how our global economy and modern lifestyles may drastically change across the coming years. We watch as the weather patterns shift in dramatic ways with global warming, and as species become extinct through the effects of human pollution and over-population. Our world as we have known it is radically changing.

Many of us react to these changes with either despair or denial. We feel helpless in the face of the magnitude of the challenges that surround us. Some of us work hard through activism to call attention to the current global crises and to help us reorient our lives to make meaningful changes. This response is evident in the work of many scientists and environmentalists concerned with global warming and in the peace activists who see our need to unite and collaborate as a global community. Others of us try to deal with the challenges by exerting even more effort to be in control and to cling to old ways of being. This response was apparent, for example, in many of the policies and actions of the Bush/Cheney administration in the United States following the crisis of September 11, 2001. Yet, these types of efforts only exacerbate our problems, as we saw in the increase in terrorism and mistrust of the United States around the world in the past several years. As we noted in the myth of Sedna, the father's effort to regain control and to take back his daughter led to disaster and to her death.

Rather than clinging to the past, we need to, following Sedna's example, dare to have the courage to step out of the cultural norms as Sedna followed Raven into the wilderness, into the unknown, setting her life on a new course. We do not know where this path of transformation may lead, but we have to trust that we are held by larger powers and forces that are beyond our comprehension. While we are making conscious choices and taking the steps that we can in positive ways to address our current issues, we also need to be open to new ways of consciousness and radically new ways of being.

This path also means preparing ourselves for the changes that are occurring on a global level environmentally, economically, politically, and socially. It is important that we not expect the old forms and systems of government and business to continue as they have across the past few hundred years. What we have relied on as our external sources of security have been bound to a way of being that has exploited the resources of our world and led us to the brink of disaster. We need to divest ourselves of our attachment to and dependence on that way of life.

How do we follow this path? As Pluto speaks to us of the death of old ways of being and knowing, we realize that our guidance will not come through the religious forms or beliefs of the past or through the dictates of political or even spiritual leaders. It will not come from outside of us or from some power over us or external authority. We will not find our way by exerting even more control and dominance over others or over the natural environment. The ancient wisdom of the past and the findings of modern quantum physics tell us that everything is interconnected, and that the path to healing is through finding and knowing the center within ourselves and in recognizing the consciousness in all of life and the source, the unity, from which we all come.

What we have realized from our journey through time and across space is that the universe is sentient. We may call this spirit or energy, and this soul of the cosmos is speaking to us through the patterns of the sky and of the Earth in each moment. This means we need to learn the way of deep listening and intuition, attuning to the whisper of spirit and the wisdom of our own bodies. It means finding the center within, the divinity that resides in each one of us. It means learning to discern truth from illusion and continually refining our ability to see and hear what is all around us. This truth resides in the patterns of the stars, the shape of a flower, or the movement of a bird, and it lives in our own hearts. The center, the source, the knowing, is within us as well as in all of life.

If we begin to live in compassion, from the heart, the path to that knowing will deepen, and we will begin to understand the truth of our interconnectedness and oneness with all of life. As Thomas Berry asserts, this is the challenge of moving into the new "Ecozoic Era," in which we remember that we live in communion with all of life rather than relating to the world around us as objects to be exploited (see Berry, *The Great Work: Our Way into the Future,* p. 8). To do this, we have to come back into deeper connection with our hearts.

Recent research has shown that our heart actually has neurotransmitters, much like our brains (see Pearsall, *The Heart's Code: Tapping the Wisdom and Power of Our Heart Energy,* p. 68). These researchers have found that we tap into our intuition and most effective decision-making abilities not by linear analysis with our minds but rather by attuning to our hearts. In this way, the brain is entrained by the heart and knows how to respond, rather than the mind dominating and entraining the heart, which results in confusion, stress, and illness as well as disconnection from the body and from the natural world.

By learning to listen to our inner knowing and our heart's awareness (living from our center, attuned to the center of the universe), we will learn what it means to be in right relationship with ourselves and with all of life. The Sedna story is one wisdom tale about the importance of right relationship. As we have seen, it is a myth coming to us from the Inuit people, and it speaks deeply of their awareness that to live and thrive, they needed to honor and be in right relationship with the land and sea around them. The myth relates how their relationship with the Arctic Sea, their source of life and sustenance, was not as a resource to be managed or exploited, but as an entity to honor and respect.

This relationship was manifested in the act of gratitude and reverence after the first catch of a fish when the fisherman would spill drops of fresh water into the mouth of the fish and give thanks to Sedna, the mother of the sea creatures. The story also emphasizes that Sedna observed how the fish and sea creatures were treated after being killed for the food and clothing for the people. If they were treated with respect, she would be pleased. If not, the people could expect her punishment through deprivation of fish or through storms. The meaning of this story is clear; we experience direct consequences in relation to how we treat the natural world around us and its creatures. We see that now in the consequences of global warming and the diseases resulting from the toxins in the environment. So, a deep part of the message of the Earth and the sky in this time is our need to return to right relationship with each other and with the world around us.

What does that mean? How do we live in right relationship?

Imagine living as if everything around you was alive and sentient. Imagine experiencing the rock in your garden, the tree on the side of the street, the squirrel running up the tree, and yourself as equal in value. Think how differently you might live. If we lived this way, we would no longer view our natural environment or others, or even our own bodies, as objects to be controlled and used. Instead, we would learn to live in reverence, respect, and gratitude. We would begin to truly see and listen again. Everything around us would be seen and known as a celebration and manifestation of the spirit, the energy that is in all of life, in all that exists. When we sat down to dinner, we would feel deep gratitude for the animals and plants that gave of themselves for our sustenance. When we walked outside, we would be aware of how our actions brought life or harm to the creatures and environment around us. Imagine what it would be like to live in right relationship with all that we encounter, acting out of gratitude and wonder rather than out of disconnection, fear, exploitation, or abuse. The message of the Earth and sky to us in this time is that we can no longer afford to live a life of disconnection, dominance and denial. We must let go of our past patterns, or we will bear the consequences of that and face our own possible extinction.

A friend of mine was on a business trip a few weeks ago. As she sat on the airplane, she overheard a few other businesspeople discussing global warming. One laughingly said to the others that she had heard that global warming was all a big hoax. The others agreed, and all laughed together. When I heard this story, my heart broke. What I realized is how drastic the disconnection of our culture from our natural world has become. We do not need the evidence of scientists or the dictates of politicians to tell us what is real. All we need to do is live in relationship with Earth, and we will feel and know how drastically the weather patterns have changed and how these changes are affecting the animals and plants and ourselves.

The story of Sedna and the wisdom of the sky are guiding us back into connection. We can begin to connect just by taking twenty minutes each day to walk in the neighborhood or woods or fields where we live and to begin to observe the trees, plants, and animals that share our immediate environment. All we need to do is to begin to open our eyes and ears to what is right in front of us, to begin to step back into relationship again.

Another way to begin to come back into connection with the natural world is to begin to pay more attention to our bodies. Our physical bodies are our link to the natural world. Also, how we treat our bodies parallels how we treat the Earth. If we are burning ourselves out, disregarding our own health, and overriding the messages from our bodies, we are doing to ourselves what we have been doing to our environment. If we pay attention to our own bodies and begin to honor them as sacred, we will already be on the path to coming back into right relationship with the natural world.

Another step that we can take is to begin to let go of patriarchal and hierarchical ways of thinking and being. Since the time of Aries, these underlying assumptions and the patterns based on them have pervaded our lives. Imagine what it would be like to go into work and to realize that your boss is no more important than you are, nor your employee any less important. What if we treated each of them with the respect that we long for ourselves? What if we treated each person, as well as each life form that we encounter, in that way? Imagine how different our world would become. We can begin that process by living with more awareness of how we step into or out of these hierarchical patterns or power dynamics in our day-to-day lives.

As we work with what it means to be in right relationship, we come to a deeper sense of respect and compassion for the world around us. At the same time, we also begin to integrate the difference between rules and human laws, and right action and natural law. Our current cultural context gives us regulations and laws that we must obey or face punishment. We need human laws to provide guidelines and protections for us within our human societies; yet we need to honor natural law to guide us in living in relationship with the conscious, living world around us.

What if we lived in a way that we honored natural law as much as human law? What if we tuned in to the consequences of our actions and their effects on the world in which we reside? We would, for example, not pollute our yards with pesticides – not because there might be a regulation against it, but because we would understand the natural consequence of poisoning our environment and the plants and animals around us, as well as our own illnesses that would result.

Living in natural law and right action does not mean being a passive victim of circumstances or sacrificing oneself out of false compassion. It means living with passion and consciousness, discerning in each moment what is right action. This means living in a more complex manner, with the awareness of the interconnectedness of all of life. Living in right action means having the spectrum of choices before us and living with consciousness, rather than operating out of fear, hatred, or blind allegiance to external authority. It means living and acting with passion from the heart and with full awareness of the consequences of our actions and the interconnectedness of our lives with all that is around us, even with those who might be different from us or those who might wish us harm. We are all part of the whole. This is the deeper message of Sedna.

Sedna dissolved into her unity with the sea and the sea creatures. She was human and fish and seal and seaweed. We are not separate. We are all a part of the web of life, and our form, our current incarnation, is fleeting and fluid. I am a woman residing in the United States today; yet in the past or in the future, I may be the tree outside my window or the stone in the garden or the young terrorist from another country struggling to find meaning in a broken world. If we live in that awareness and sense of unity, it changes every moment of our lives and every decision that we make and every action that we take.

Another message of Sedna and of the Age of Aquarius is that everything is energy. Dualism is an illusion. There is no separate self and other, male and female, up and down, in and out. All are parts of the larger whole. This is the meaning of the understanding in modern physics that matter is not fixed; all life "foams" in and out of being. If we could begin to live that awareness, our need for external tangible security and a fixed sense of identity would dissipate, and our fear of death would dissolve. Differences of belief systems, religions, nationalities, ethnic backgrounds, sexual orientation, gender, or socioeconomic status would continue to exist, but as differing manifestations of an underlying unity rather than as a basis for division, separation, hatred, fear, and polarity. This is the primary message of Uranus and the Aquarian Age – calling us into a true understanding of community and egalitarian relationships and the common energy that permeates all of life.

In moving beyond polarity, we also come to realize that the sacred, the numinous, spirit, is not transcendent or immanent. It is not outside us or only within us. It is both/and. To fully step into our divinity, to dissolve into that sense of the sacred in all of life, is to move into humility and to honor what is Divine in everything. It is to realize that we are thirty-thousand light years from the source and center of our galaxy, which has birthed us and formed us, and the center is also within each one of us and in each object and creature that shares our universe.

In moving beyond this polarity, it also means no longer engaging in the dialectic between a masculine god and a female goddess or one God and a multiplicity of deities. It means embracing the sacred feminine, which teaches us that spirit is embodied and is in all of life and that we are born from the womb of a woman and the black womb of the universe. We live in the mystery of the sacred dark energy of the universe, and we are surrounded by the wisdom of the darkness and the potentiality of the fecund void. At the same time, we also reach for the sky god, the deity beyond the realm of the tangible, and we seek enlightenment and revere the light and energy of action and manifestation. We honor the sacred that is incarnate and transcendent, yin and yang, fire and water, earth and air, within and without. Spirit is in all yet beyond all. This is unity consciousness.

The Earth and sky are speaking to us and calling us back to this deeper wisdom and awareness. If we listen, perhaps we will come back into right relationship, find our center, and begin to live out of a galactic and embodied consciousness beyond anything we have ever known.

AFTERWORD:

CIRCLES WITHIN CIRCLES

Circles within circles
A breathing, swirling spiral,
This galaxy, our home.
In the center,
Pulses a black hole,
The dark womb,
Birthing stars.
All life arises from the
Sea of chaos and darkness.

We come from the fecund void,
Stardust singing in our bones.
We are of the sky and of the Earth,
The pulse of the universe
Courses through our veins.
The energy of creation
Weaves a web that holds the stars and planets
And moves in the cells of our bodies.

When we no longer hear the song of the universe
And the drumbeat of Mother Earth
We sever our connections with the Earth and sky
And cut our umbilical cord to source.
We drift in time and space

And lose our way
And our sense of who we are
And who we have been.

It is time to remember
To reweave the web
To hear anew the singing of the stars
And the heart-beat of the Earth.
It is time to open once again
To the wisdom of the sky and Earth.
Following the path of the labyrinth,
We find our center, our source,
The womb of the Earth and of the sky,
And are birthed anew.

BIBLIOGRAPHY

Baigent, Michael. *From the Omens of Babylon: Astrology and Ancient Mesopotamia.* London: Arkana, Penguin Books, 1994.

Baillie, Mike. *Exodus to Arthur: Catastrophic Encounters with Comets.* London: B. T. Batsford LTD, 2003.

Baring, Anne and Jules Cashford. *The Myth of the Goddess: Evolution of an Image.* London: Viking Press, 1991.

Bauval, Robert and Adrian Gilbert. *The Orion Mystery.* New York: Three Rivers Press, 1994.

Berry, Thomas. *The Dream of the Earth.* San Francisco: Sierra Club Books, 1988.

Berry, Thomas. *The Great Work: Our Way into the Future.* New York: Bell Tower Press, 1999.

Brady, Bernadette. *Brady's Book of Fixed Stars.* York Beach, Maine: Samuel Weiser, Inc., 1998.

Burt, Kathleen. *Archetypes of the Zodiac.* St. Paul, Minnesota: Llewellyn Publications, 1993.

Capra, Fritjof, *The Web of Life.* New York: Anchor Books, Doubleday, 1996.

Casey, Carolyn. *Making the Gods Work for You: The Astrological Language of the Psyche*. New York: Harmony Press, 1998.

Cashford, Jules. *The Moon: Myth and Image*. New York: Four Walls Eight Windows, 2003.

Childre, Doc Lew and Howard Martin. *The Heartmath Solution*. New York: HarperOne, 2000.

Clavin, Whitney. "Planet-Like Body Discovered at Fringes of Our Solar System." nasa.gov.

Collins, Andrew. *The Cygnus Mystery: Unlocking the Ancient Secret of Life's Origins in the Cosmos*. London: Watkins Publishing LTD, 2007.

Clube, Victor and Bill Napier. *The Cosmic Serpent*. New York: Universe Publishing, 1982.

Cruttenden, Walter. *Lost Star of Myth and Time*. Pittsburgh, Pennsylvania: St. Lynn's Press, 2005.

Cruttenden, Walter. "Precession of the Equinox: The Ancient Truth Behind Celestial Motion." binaryresearchinstitute.org.

Dalley, Stephanie. *Myths from Mesopotamia*. London: Oxford University Press, 1989.

Dames, Michael. *Mythic Ireland*. London: Thames and Hudson, 1992.

de Santillana, Giorgio and Hertha von Dechend. *Hamlet's Mill*. Boston: David R. Godine, Publisher, 1977.

Friedel, David and Linda Schele and Joy Parker. *Maya Cosmos*. New York: William Morrow and Co, Inc., 1993.

George, Demetra, *Mysteries of the Dark Moon: The Healing Power of the Goddess*. New York: HarperCollins, 1992.

Gimbutas, Marija. *The Civilization of the Goddess*. New York: HarperSanFrancisco, Harper Collins, 1991.

Gimbutas, Marija. *The Language of the Goddess*. San Francisco: Harper & Row, 1989.

Gleadow, Rupert. *The Origin of the Zodiac*. New York: Castle Books, 1968.

Grasse, Ray. *Signs of the Times*. Charlottesville, Virginia: Hampton Roads Publishing Company, 2002.

Green, Jeff, "Astrological Ages and Sub-Ages." evolutionaryastrology. net.

Green, Jeff. *Pluto: The Evolutionary Journey of the Soul*, vol. I. St. Paul, Minnesota: Llewellyn Publications, 1996.

Green, Jeff. *Pluto: The Soul's Journey Through Relationships*, vol. II. St. Paul, Minnesota: Llewellyn Publications, 1997.

Green, Jeff. *Uranus: Freedom from the Known*. St. Paul, Minnesota: Llewellyn Publications, 1989.

Greene, Liz. *The Astrological Neptune and the Quest for Redemption*. York Beach, Maine: Samuel Weiser, Inc., 1996.

Guttman, Ariel and Kenneth Johnson. *Mythic Astrology*. St. Paul, Minnesota: Llewellyn Publications, 1993.

Hancock, Graham and Robert Bauval. *The Message of the Sphinx: A Quest for the Hidden Legacy of Mankind*. New York: Three Rivers Press, 1997.

Hancock, Graham. *Fingerprints of the Gods.* Portsmouth, New Hampshire: William Heinemann Ltd, 1996.

Hancock, Graham. *Underworld: The Mysterious Origins of Civilization.* New York: Three Rivers Press, 2002.

Hand, Robert. "History of Astrology – Another View." accessnewage. com.

Holy Bible, New International Version. Grand Rapids, Michigan: Zondervan Bible Publishers, 1978.

Jacobsen, Thorkild. *The Treasures of Darkness: A History of Mesopotamian Religion.* New Haven and London: Yale University Press, 1976.

Jenkins, John Major. *Galactic Alignment: The Transformation of Consciousness According to Mayan, Egyptian, and Vedic Traditions.* Rochester, Vermont: Bear & Co, 2002.

Jenkins, John Major and Terrence McKenna. *Maya Cosmogenesis 2012.* Rochester, Vermont: Bear & Company, 1998.

Jung, C. G. *The Archetypes and the Collective Unconscious.* Translated by RFC Hull, New York: Princeton University Press, 1969.

Kramer, Samuel Noah. *Sumerian Mythology.* Philadelphia, Pennsylvania: University of Pennsylvania Press, 1961.

Krupp, E. C. *In Search of Ancient Astronomies.* Garden City, New York: Doubleday & Co., 1978.

Lash, John. *Quest for the Zodiac: The Cosmic Code Beyond Astrology.* Loughborough, Leicestershire, Great Britain: Thoth Publications, 1999.

Marshack, Alexander. *The Roots of Civilization*. London: Weidenfeld & Nicolson, 1972.

Melia, Fulvio. *The Black Hole at the Center of Our Galaxy*. Princeton and Oxford: Princeton University Press, 2003.

Michell, John. *At the Center of the World*. London: Thames and Hudson, 1994.

Neumann, Erich. *The Origins and History of Consciousness*. Princeton, NY: Princeton 1954.

Noble, Vicki. *The Double Goddess: Women Sharing Power*. Rochester, Vermont: Bear & Company, 2003.

Ohno, Susumu, MD. "So Much 'Junk DNA' in our Genome." Brookhaven Symposium on Biology, 1972.

Pearsall, Paul, PhD. *The Heart's Code: Tapping the Wisdom and Power of Our Heart Energy*. New York: Broadway Books, 1998.

Peiser, Benny. "Comets and Disaster in the Bronze Age." *Journal of the Council of British Archeology*, December 1997.

Perera, Sylvia Brinton. *Descent to the Goddess*. Toronto, Canada: Inner City Books, 1981.

Pink, Daniel. *A Whole New Mind: Moving from the Information Age to the Conceptual Age*. New York: Penguin Group, 2005.

Qitsualik, Rachel. *Nunatsiaq News*. March 19, 2004.

Qitsualik, Rachel. *Nunatsiaq News*. June 27, 2003.

Rudhyar, Dane. *The Galactic Dimension of Astrology: The Sun is Also a Star*. Sante Fe, New Mexico: Aurora Press, 1982.

Ruggles, Clive. *Ancient Astronomy: An Encyclopedia of Cosmologies and Myth*. Santa Barbara, California: ABC-CLIO, Inc., 2005.

Shlain, Leonard. *The Alphabet versus the Goddess*. New York: Penguin Group, 1999.

Schore, Allan. *Affect Regulation and the Origin of the Self.* Hillsdale, New York: Lawrence Erlbaum Associates, Publishers, 1994.

Swimme, Brian. *The Hidden Heart of the Cosmos*. Maryknoll, New York: Orbis Books, 1996.

Swimme, Brian and Thomas Berry. *The Universe Story*. New York: HarperCollins, 1992.

Tarnas, Richard. *Cosmos and Psyche*. New York: Viking, Penguin Group, 2006.

Tarnas, Richard. *Prometheus, the Awakener*. Putnam, Connecticut: Spring Publications, Inc., 1995.

Temple, Robert. *The Sirius Mystery*. Rochester, Vermont: Destiny Books, 1998.

Tindol, Robert. "The Dwarf Planet Formerly Known as Xena Has Officially Been Named Eris, IAU Announces." Press release, Caltech.edu, September 14, 2006.

van Gennep, Arnold. *The Rites of Passage*. Chicago: University of Chicago Press, 1960.

Vidler, Mark. *The Star Mirror*. London: Thorsons Press, Hammersmith, 1998.

Villoldo, Alberto, PhD. *Shaman, Healer, Sage*. New York: Harmony Books, 2000.

Walker, Barbara. *The Woman's Encyclopedia of Myths and Secrets.* San Francisco, New York: HarperSanFrancisco, 1983.

Wolkstein, Diane and Samuel Noah Kramer. *Inanna: Queen of Heaven and Earth.* New York: Harper & Row Publishers, 1983.

Zimmer, Heinrich. "Man and Transformation." *Eranos*, Equinox Press, 2008

Lightning Source UK Ltd.
Milton Keynes UK
UKHW011123210322
400384UK00001B/123